LIFE CRAFTING

Create the Life You Were Meant to Live

Other Books by the Author

What's Your Story?
What's Your Career?

LIFE CRAFTING

Create the Life You Were Meant to Live

DR. CLYDE W. EKBOM
Licensed Psychologist, Mental Health Counselor

Life Crafting
Create the Life You Were Meant to Live

Copyright © 2007 Clyde Ekbom. All rights reserved. No part of this book may be reproduced or retransmitted in any form or by any means without the written permission of the publisher.

Published by Wheatmark™
610 East Delano Street, Suite 104, Tucson, Arizona 85705 U.S.A.
www.wheatmark.com

International Standard Book Number: 9781587368301
Library of Congress Control Number: 2007924863

ACKNOWLEDGEMENTS

I want to thank my students at the University of Minnesota-Duluth and the University of Wisconsin-Superior. Without my interactions with you all as I formed my thoughts and ideas (and tried them out on you!), I could never have written this book. Good luck to you all and go out there and MAKE A DIFFERENCE!

To my wife, Andrea, who trudged off to a job she hated every day as I stayed home and wrote:

To my daughter, Talia, who really didn't understand what I was doing at home all day, but loved me anyway:

To my "editors"—Andrea, Jeff, and Gene—whose sage advice saved my readers a lot of aggravation.

THANK YOU!

How to Contact the Author

As I am in the process of moving, the only reliable way to contact me at this time is via my e-mail address: souldoc1@msn.com. My website should be up and running soon.

Once my website is established, I intend to accept select clients for consulting or coaching, as needed. The concepts in the book are clear, I believe, but not always easy to carry out on one's own. For the time being, contact me by e-mail. I respond to all personal letters and e-mail.

CONTENTS

Preface 1

Introduction 3

Part 1: Three Lives 5

1. Bill's past 7
2. Anne's past 15
3. Mary's past 21
4. The nature of human change 26
5. Survival: no change, no adjustment, no growth 32
6. Adjustment: change, but external only 36
7. Growth: change, internal & external 39
8. The courage to change 44

Part 2, Alternative 1: How about you? 51

9. Comparisons 53
10. Home 61
11. School and other people 66

12. Society 70
13. Take your pick 73
14. Who are you, really? 76
Conclusion 87

Part 2, Alternative 2:   How about you? 89
9.   Comparisons 91
10. Home 99
11. School and other people 104
12. Society 108
13. Take your pick 111
14. Who are you, really? 114
Conclusion 118
Bibliography 121
How to order 122
About the Author 125

PREFACE

In my 20 plus years as a professor and psychologist, I've found that most people's problems have their origin in non-acceptance of their authentic selves. For a variety of reasons, they find important parts of themselves repugnant to other people so they create, for public consumption, a false self that they believe is more socially acceptable. The effect is that people, maybe all their lives, act as if they are someone they're not. The result is that they become someone other than they were intended to be and the world never receives the contribution they were supposed to make.

What's ironic is that, in therapy, the more they are able to identify, own and show who they really are, the more interesting and appealing they become (to me as well as to those around them)--certainly more interesting and appealing, and "human," than their facade ever was. The purpose of this book is to help you identify, own and become in your own life the beautiful person that you are and were meant to be.

The first half of the book (**Part 1**) tells the stories of three people (all of whom are composites of people I have known) which, I believe are illustrative of the lives of people who live in the United States in the first part of the 21st Century. The experiences and decisions attributed to the three as well as the lives they lead, although fictitious, are true representations of what I've seen in therapy.

The second half of the book (**Part 2**) is designed to help you to draw, from the lives of the three, lessons to be applied to your own life, lessons that I hope will help you make of yourself what you were meant to be.

*Note: This book is written from the male point of view to avoid the awkward "he/she" construction of a balanced, male/female perspective. My message is meant to apply to both genders—no slight is intended to anyone.

INTRODUCTION

I want to introduce you to three people who, like all of us, are trying to make sense of their lives.

Bill

Bill Jones is a well-respected orthopedic surgeon at a prominent hospital in the Midwest. He comes from a long line of medical doctors. His grandfather was one, as was his father. Family history has it that one of his ancestors was a surgeon in the Civil War. Bill is married, has two children and lives in the "best" part of his city. Bill's occupation and good reputation have secured for him and his family a very comfortable existence. He often says, somewhat ironically, that he "has it all."

Anne

Anne Peters is an associate at a department store in a medium-sized city in the Eastern United States. She is divorced and has one child, aged 15. Anne comes from a large household—three boys and four girls—that was managed in much the same way her Mother's was back in Germany before she met and married Anne's American soldier father. Anne loves her child but finds her work at the store, and her life in general, boring and her future dim. While she gets help from her parents, she barely makes ends meet and carries more guilt than she'll admit to about her child not having the clothes and "extras" that Anne herself was denied when she was growing up and that caused her so much pain.

Mary

Mary Arthur is unemployed and lives with her boyfriend who works in the evenings as a bouncer at a local tavern in a large metropolitan area in the Southwest. She spends most of her time hanging out with other unmarried girlfriends--mostly younger, but in similar circumstances—talking and helping them take care of their kids. If there is any alcohol or other drugs available, Mary will indulge, but no longer to the extent of the others who, she knows all too well, do it to dull the pain of their lives. Mary is slowly coming to realize that she wants a family of her own and that she doesn't want to raise her kids the way she sees her friend's kids being raised--and certainly not the way she herself was raised.

Although Bill, Anne and Mary are quite different people with different backgrounds and experiences, they have at least one thing in common. All are unhappy and unfulfilled in their present lives and are ready for a change.

What follows is a look back at what brought these three individuals to their present circumstances and what they do to transform their lives

PART 1

Three Lives

CHAPTER 1

Bill's past

Upbringing

Bill's parents are Dan and Susan Jones.

Bill's parents had two children: Bill and his younger sister, Julie. Bill's mother, Susan, remembers both of her children as being bright and energetic. Bill in particular was a "ball of fire" she remembers, interested in everything and always on the go. Their family was such that Susan stayed home and took care of the kids while Dan, Bill's dad, was a self-employed physician in general practice with five other doctors in a clinic jointly built and owned by the six partners. The effect of this arrangement was that Bill saw much more of his mother than his dad. When he could, however, Dan spent time with Bill, teaching him what it was to be a man and what the world was like and that, incidentally, being a medical doctor was an especially good way to make a living, and a life. Bill much admired his father and, from a young age, spent much of his spare time in his dad's office amongst all the interesting stuff and mysterious smells that made up the medical environment. Although Dan was wary of pushing his son into the medical field, he was pleased, and showed it, at Bill's apparent interest. Bill loved it when Dan would tell interesting stories of his own father, also a doctor, in the day when doctors made house calls, day and night and in all kinds of weather.

Susan and Dan had a good marriage. They loved, cared for and respected one another and worked well in partnership to raise their two children. Family rules for the children were clear and consistent and the kids knew that each parent would enforce them and back one another up in decisions made regarding the management of the children and the household. While their home was a busy place, and neither child felt that they got enough of their father, Bill and Julie felt loved and respected by their parents.

Early Schooling

Bill's parents—though they could have afforded to send him to private school—decided that, seeing as how Bill had plans to be a doctor and was eventually going to have patients from all walks of life, sent him to public school. Bill loved school and thrived in it. He was a unique individual in that he was a fierce competitor in sports, hating more than almost anything to lose, while off the field he was a gentle and caring friend and companion to all. He had a steady girlfriend two years younger than he was whom he dated from his sophomore year on.

Bill was especially good at football and was the "star" of his high school team that went to state his senior year, winning runners-up honors. Bill was offered several football scholarships, but (in consultation with his father) decided that it would take too much of his time, and admission to medical school was very competitive. Furthermore, Bill's father argued that playing football at that level would present too great a risk of injury to his hands, vital to a doctor's success. Bill contented himself with high school athletics alone.

Bill's teachers and administrators admired Bill's all-around ability and drive and treated him with caring and respect. They let him know that they appreciated him and communicated to him that he had a great future ahead of him. Although they were aware that his father was a physician and that it was Bill's ambition to be one too, they let him know that they believed that he was capable of being anything he wanted to be.

Throughout high school, Bill was treated by his parents as an autonomous, intelligent human being. He was allowed to make decisions commensurate with his age and maturity level and their perception of his ability to handle the consequences of his actions. As he got older and more sure of himself, Bill was given more and more latitude in his behaviors. Bill's parents never had any reason to regret the trust they had placed in him. His mother remembers that they "didn't have to worry about him at all" during his high school years.

All-in-all, Bills K-12 schooling experience confirmed for him what he had learned about himself at home, that he was a worthy and loveable individual and that he was capable of making decisions in his life that led to positive consequences. Upon graduation, Bill was voted by his classmates "most likely to succeed" as well as "nicest to be around."

It is at the time of high school graduation that young people are forced, perhaps for the first time, to face their future. The comfort and security of home and school are about to be withdrawn, and they are now expected to make it on their own. The inevitable question, "What are you going to do after graduation?" is a scary but, at the same time, an exciting one to try to answer.

Before one can answer, " I'm going to be a _____," a great deal of thought is required, thought based upon one's perception of himself and of the world and where he might fit in that world. How does he acquire information on such a topic? Well, he must look at his experiences to date, particularly how he has been treated by important others and how he "stacks up" to his peers, both in "looks" and in "smarts," because he knows that he must, all his life, compete against them and their like for mates and jobs.

The answer to the "I'm going to be" question is found in answers to two preliminary queries, and one general assessment: Am I loveable, Am I capable, and Am I adequate or fit for life. Answers to these questions come from one's experiences at home and in school: Did my parents and other important adults love and respect me? Did I have good friends or "chums" who accepted me for who I was? Was I well or ill received by my classmates and teachers in school—in short, was I popular? Was I able to perform the tasks necessary for "success" in high school—in short, was I smart?

With answers to the lovable/capable questions, he generally makes an assessment of his overall adequacy or fitness for life, in comparison to other people his age. From here he is able to make an estimate of the "quality" of his probable mate and career over his lifetime, as well as his overall lifestyle. These, then, become his goals and his answer to: What **am** I going to do after graduation?

Please note that, as portrayed, the above self-assessment seems a deliberate, step-by-step process. It most assuredly is not. I describe it in this way for illustrative purposes only. First of all, the process itself usually takes place somewhere below the level of consciousness. Secondly, one usually goes through all the steps described, but not in any particular order, and probably not one time only. Finally, the intensity with which people go through the process varies with each individual. In fact, some people choose to put off deliberations of this kind altogether by mindlessly following the crowd going, for example, to college or the armed services.

From Bill's reading of how his parents, his chums as well as other trusted adults treated him as he was growing up, he concluded that he was perceived by them as being a likeable person with good human qualities. He read the same from his classmates, plus he felt that they found him **physically attractive** to the opposite sex (a big part of "lovable" for 18-year-olds). With these thoughts in mind, he answered a strong "yes" to "Are you lovable."

From his accomplishments, starting at home and extending to school (particularly, did people consider him **smart**—a big part of "capable" for 18-year-olds) and his ability to apprehend his needs and, by his reasoned choices, satisfy them in his life, he answered another strong "yes" to capable. Adding all this information up, he concluded that he was, indeed, adequate or fit for life; he could make it on his own—not in the sense that he wouldn't want or need help and guidance from others from time-to-time, but that he didn't need someone to **tell** him how to live. He felt strong enough to figure this out on his own. Armed with this information he answered the three vital life questions, those that determine our goals in life, as follows:

> Who am I?: both lovable and capable; able to acquire the good things in life, and well deserving of them.
>
> What's the world like?: a benign and exciting place where I am welcomed and invited to make my contribution, wherever I see fit.
>
> What's my place in the world?: the top: anywhere I want to go but, in all probability, as an M.D.

Later Schooling

There was never any question that Bill would go to college, and so he did. Bill whisked through his undergraduate program in school. He enjoyed almost all his classes, even those that had nothing to do with medicine. He was surprised, for example, at how much he liked his religion, psychology and philosophy classes. His favorite professor, in fact, was his psychology professor who took a particular interest in him, even to the point of suggesting that Bill should consider a future in psychology. Bill was knocked off stride by this as his path had always been laid out for him and he, and his father, counted on his becoming a general practitioner. Nevertheless, he had a long talk with his father about the possibility of becoming a psychiatrist. His father listened but advised Bill to stay on his present course. Psychiatry, he said, is a "soft" science that was difficult to get a grasp on. You could never really know whether you helped anyone or not. Not so, with "real" science where disease or trauma was either there or it wasn't and you could tell almost immediately whether you were right or not in your diagnosis and treatment of patients. After some thought, Bill agreed, and pushed psychiatry out of the front of his mind.

Bill finished his undergraduate degree and went off to medical school. He did well in all his classes, enjoying almost all of them. Not surprisingly, his psychiatry rotation interested him the most. The workings of the human mind were infinitely fascinating to him and he spent hours talking to similarly interested classmates, some of whom were considering becoming psychiatrists. Bill felt drawn to it himself, but he reasoned that he was too close now to finishing to switch course. Furthermore, his dad was anxious to step down so he could pursue retirement interests in travel and was counting on Bill to take over for him. Bill went on to graduate third in his class.

Work & Life

Bill interned at a prominent hospital in his home town and, indeed, joined his father's practice. His father stepped down and he and Bill's mom traveled the world until he died unexpectedly of a heart attack. Bill was devastated, but even more determined to carry on the legacy of his father and grandfather.

Bill married Nancy, a nurse that he had met previously in his residency, and they soon started a family. From the start, the clinic thrived, in no small part to Bill who threw himself into his work and the business of the clinic. He was well-liked and well-respected by his patients and co-workers, and prospered.

After ten years or so of this, however, Bill started to get bored. As a result, he decided—with a good measure of guilt as he suspected his father would not have approved—to leave the clinic and become an orthopedic surgeon, mainly because sports-related injuries, especially bone and ligament trauma, were of most interest to him. He knew that his career needed a shot of adrenaline, and he believed orthopedics would be that shot.

After training in orthopedics, he ended up in a large hospital with more money, prestige, and more patients than he could handle. After only three years of this, however, he again got that same "bored" and "is this all there is" feeling that had driven him out of the clinic that his dad had been so proud of. Furthermore, he came to the realization that his home life wasn't much better than his work life.

He was disappointed that his wife seemed to care only about decorating and redecorating the house and joining the circle of the "right" people in town. He felt that he didn't know his kids and only saw them when they wanted money from him to buy whatever it was that kids were into at the time.

He went into a fit of depression that centered on questions such as: "What's wrong with me? I have a great job; I'm loved, respected. I have a beautiful wife and healthy kids. I have all the stuff I'll ever need. Yet, I'm not satisfied. Is there something wrong with me that I can't appreciate what just about anyone I know would trade their own circumstances to have?"

Despite his efforts to "snap out of it," Bill grew more and

more disinterested in his work and his family. People looked the other way for a time, but then couldn't help but notice that there was something wrong with Bill. Rumors at the hospital were that there was trouble at home. At home, his wife couldn't figure out what was going on. "Where's my husband," she asked herself. "He used to enjoy being home, going to parties, helping me redecorate, participate with the kids."

For a time, she was sympathetic, trying to help, and when that didn't work, suggesting he go to someone else for help. He didn't go. After that, she got scared and filled with her own, more personal questions: "What's wrong? Is it me? What if he doesn't snap out of this? He's going to get fired! Am I going to have to go back to work again? Does he still love me? Is he having an affair?"

Bill, all the while, was trying to figure out what was going on, too. He had always been so successful, so sure of himself: "What is wrong with me," he would say to himself. "Could Nancy be right? Am I going crazy? I'm hurting my family, my mother." After a "buck yourself up" session like this, he would do better for a time, but his doubts and his lethargy always came back. And at those times, he could always picture his father gazing at him with a stern look, shaking his head with disapproval.

Bill was in trouble. For the first time he was questioning himself, his ability to cope with life on his own. His colleagues and friends were starting to stay away from him. Even his wife and kids were starting to avoid him when they could. The life he had built for himself and his family was crumbling. What he thought would make him happy, made him miserable. He was questioning his judgment and ability to apprehend reality and respond to it favorably.

CHAPTER 2

Anne's past

Upbringing

Anne's parents are Gertrude and Patrick Peters.

When Anne was growing up, Gertrude and Patrick were dairy farmers. When they started the farm, and when the first kids (for a total of six), including Anne, were young, they were very poor. There was always plenty to eat and the kids were always adequately clothed, albeit with hand-me-downs, but there was little left for extras. The family became experts at making-do. The kids were required to help out on the farm, either in the barn with Dad or in the house with Mom. And it was not just to teach them the value of hard labor (although that was important to them, too); it was out of economic necessity that the children worked. Anne's parents simply could not do it all by themselves and couldn't afford to hire help. The kids pitched in gladly, for the most part, and have mostly happy memories of those times.

But the older kids (Anne was the oldest) did miss out on outside activities that they longed to participate in. Anne, for example, begged to take piano lessons, but there simply wasn't enough extra money at the time for her to do so. It was only the 5th and 6th children who were allowed "extras" because, by the time they were of age, much of the start-up work was done and labor-saving devices installed and the farm was running smoothly and prospering. Anne would have liked to have joined some clubs, the band, and gone to some dances, as well, but it wasn't to be. She had chores to do at home and the family was counting on her.

The marriage of Anne's parents was a good one. They loved each other and they loved their children. Patrick was the disciplinarian of the two--and there had to be one in that large a family in that small a house—who sometimes got a bit overzealous at the job (railing against circumstances that were really natural, growing-up things that the kids couldn't control), but all the kids got the notion that he loved them. The "love" word was never spoken by Anne's father, and any infractions of rules were quickly punished, but she always felt loved by him.

The nurturer in the house was Gertrude. She was from the Old Country in Germany, and came from a large family herself. She was a task-master, as was Patrick, but she was softer and more demonstrative of her love than was Patrick. The upshot was that Anne felt loved by both her parents and siblings, and lovable.

Anne also felt capable, but only to a point. When the boys came, the youngest two of the six, it became apparent to Anne and her sisters that boys were different. They had their chores and expectations were high for good school performance, as they were for the girls, but life expectations were different. It seemed to Anne that more was expected of them in the future than of any of the girls. Anne noticed that there was more talk of possible careers and work with the boys than the girls. It was almost as if the boys were more valuable than or preferred to the girls.

Anne was an excellent student in most of her classes and had vague dreams of being a doctor, but the discussion of it simply didn't happen at home. The unspoken expectation for the girls was that they would be married and make good wives and helpers to their husbands, but nothing beyond that. It was boys/men who had careers. Women had marriages and families. In this atmosphere, Anne's dream of a medical career slowly faded. In short, she felt loved and lovable in her home, but capable only in a limited capacity, as a wife and mother.

Early Schooling

Anne attended public school. From the start, it was obvious that she was bright. Everything seemed to come easily for her with the exception of mathematics. She was a shy girl so her friends were few, but loyal. Because of her rather over-worn clothes, she endured a good amount of teasing from certain classmates, teasing that she on the outside ignored, but on the inside, hurt her deeply.

She wanted to be more involved in after-school activities such as band, choir and some clubs like FFA and FTA but her parents insisted she was needed at home. Her life consisted of classes in school and her work and relationships with her siblings at home. Her Dad was around but usually not in the house, where her duties kept her, so she grew up with the notion that she loved her father, but was a bit afraid of him. She also felt that she didn't know him very well.

From her mother, she was learning "girl things"—how to cook, clean, sew, garden, can, bake bread--that she would need when she was a wife and mother. In school, there were some teachers that she admired, a couple of whom, she believed, liked her too. She, for a time, thought she might want to be a teacher, but that required a college education which she knew her parents couldn't afford, and wouldn't encourage anyway, and she had no way of earning on her own.

Anne's K-12 experience boiled down for her to a notion that she was cared for by her teachers and her small coterie of friends, including a couple of "boyfriends" along the way. She thought of herself as lovable to others, but in some ways only to the extent that she could do for others what they needed from her. She knew she was smart, but really had no outlet for that smartness. At times she had the temerity to believe that she was as smart as this or that boy who seemed to have such lofty aspirations in the world, but that there was no such outlet for her talents. She therefore felt somewhat capable, but that her perceived abilities were wasted because there was no apparent call for women with these abilities.

At high school graduation, to the question "Am I lovable" Anne was able to answer "yes" but only as far as her family was concerned. As far as school was concerned, she was a good student, so was liked by her teachers and administrators. She had a few close friends amongst her classmates, had even dated a couple of them, but there were also those who made fun of her clothes and her slightly overweight condition (amounting to a deficit in her physical attractiveness to the opposite sex calculation) so she gave a "yes/no" answer to this one. Totaled up, Anne was able to answer a tentative "yes" to "Am I lovable."

To answer to the question "Am I capable," Anne had to weigh her parent's judgments as to who she was and what she could do in the world against her demonstrated ability to get good grades in high school—that is, her "smarts" score. Her aspirations for a medical career were discouraged. She had been told that the best she could do in life would be to be a good helpmate, wife and mother. Her answer to "Am I capable," then, was: "yes," to a point.

On the basis of these musings, did she consider herself adequate or fit for life? Again, she answered a tentative "yes," but only with the help of her parents and, eventually, a stronger/smarter man.

Her subsequent answers to the three vital life questions:

Who am I?: a tentative "yes" to lovable and capable; able to acquire the good things in life, with help, and deserving of them.

What's the world like?: it's a man's world; women play a subservient role.

What's my place in the world?: married; with family; full-time mom.

Work & Life

After high school, Anne had no thought of higher education. She took a number of low-paying waitress jobs, finally finding a somewhat "permanent" job at a large Sears's store. Currently she works in the paint department of the store. She enjoyed the work for about a year and then it began to get stale and repetitive as had happened to her while working in other departments of the store. As she had in most of the other departments she served, she saw her current manager as arbitrary and not as smart as she was. She dreaded Sunday nights because she knew she would have to go back to her job the next morning, a job which she was increasingly seeing as below her capabilities.

All the while she duly searched for the "right guy" to marry, but couldn't find anyone like her father, her only real role model for a husband. She eventually met a guy who seemed to be interested in her for who she was. After going with him for a year or so, she discovered that she was pregnant. Against her better judgment, because she knew that she didn't love him, she married him and they had a little girl.

Soon after this, her husband had an affair and this helped her realize that not only did she not love this man, but she didn't want him to have anything to do with raising her daughter, so she divorced him and moved on.

With the responsibility of a daughter who depended upon her, the failure of her marriage, and the barrenness she foresaw of a life lived on the meager salary and lack of stimulation of her present job, Anne found herself in despair.

Nevertheless, Anne pressed on. She stayed with her job, tightened her belt and fell back on her parents for as much help and support that they could provide. Gradually, over time, things began to change. She was encountering women with children, married and unmarried, who were succeeding at work and at life. She judged herself to be at least as smart as her supervisors, most of whom had college degrees. She was starting to think that there was more room for women in the world than her parents had taught her.

CHAPTER 3

Mary's past

Upbringing

Mary's mother is Joann Arthur.

Mary doesn't know who her father is. In fact, she doesn't even know where her mother is now, or even if she is still alive. You see, Mary comes from a family that wasn't. Her parents never married, or even lived together. Her mother was never really a parent to her as she was drug addicted when Mary was conceived and born and, as far as she knows, throughout her childhood. Mary was bounced around from foster home to foster home and from residential care facility to residential care facility from the time she was 7 years old until she was 18.

She remembers that she never really made a personal connection with any one of her foster parents or siblings and with only two or three people in residential care. Most of her problems in her upbringing she attributes to the fact that her parents abandoned her and that many of her subsequent "care givers" used and abused her—emotionally, verbally, physically, and sexually.

Early Schooling

Mary's K-12 experience was as chaotic and spotty as was her home life. She spent only two-and-a-half years in public school before going to a residential day-school and, finally, to residential care proper. She acknowledges that, at that time, she didn't want to be in school, felt stupid and out-of-place, a fish-out-of-water. Everyone was better than she was. She rejected them before they could reject her. Suffice it to say that she didn't learn much, except that she didn't measure up to the other kids.

As she got older and with the consistency of residential life and the partial trust she gave to a couple of residential staff, Mary came to believe that she was worth something to someone else. She even came to believe that some of her "I'm no good" feelings came from circumstances beyond her control. She still, however, had a hard time trusting people who treated her nicely, thinking "What do they want from me?"

With the slight rise in her self-esteem, surrounded by other kids from similar backgrounds and watching how staff treated them and knowing that they cared, she started thinking that maybe she was worthy of life and, if so, she had better learn something. She started to apply herself in school and found, surprisingly, that she was pretty smart. Math came hard to her, but the other stuff was, after a while, not only easy but enjoyable. Her teachers and her peers in school started looking at her with something that looked like respect. She graduated from residential school and was released on a high note.

From lots of work on her own and on a lot of other people's parts, Mary was finally convinced that at least one or two people thought that she was ok, and not the freak of nature that she had once believed she was. She also believed, now, that her mother did love her and did her best—that is, she was abandoned not because she was so bad but because her mother was so impaired.

As to her calculation concerning "Am I attractive to the opposite sex," she didn't really care. Her experience with males to this point in her life made her want to distance herself from all males and male attention. Her self-esteem, therefore, was much higher than when she was younger but, as you shall see, it was fragile. Her assessment as to Am I lovable--a marginal, "yes." As to "Am I capable," her discovery, once she started to take schooling seriously, that most of her studies came easily and she was earning praise from her teachers and peers for good grades, helped her label herself as "smart" causing her to give herself a marginal "yes."

On the basis of these considerations, Mary believed that she was indeed adequate and fit for life. She believed that, if she was going to make it in the real world, she would have to do it alone, which she believed she could do. Still, in the back of her mind, was the nagging notion that she had fooled those who thought she was ok, and maybe herself, too.

Based on this, her tentative conclusions about her future:

Who am I?: a somewhat shaky "yes" to both lovable and capable; I've had it rough, but most of it was not my fault.

What's the world like?: it is a matter of luck—you can get lucky and sail through, or you can get unlucky, like I did, and get knocked down.

What's my place in the world?: a job where I can make enough money to live on my own, in my own place.

Work & Life

Mary, with the help of her last treatment facility, got work as a secretary and was doing quite well at the job and in her personal life, until she met Joe. Joe was a good-looking young man who was always between jobs and who had a long list of failed relationships with women. Mary--who missed the close, loving contact she had received in residential treatment and longed for someone to love her--saw this quite early on, but stayed with him anyway, blaming herself for his lazy, drinking and womanizing ways. "If only I love him better," she would say to herself, "he will see that I'm the woman for him and he will love me like I love him."

It wasn't to be. The more Mary tried to love him, the more elusive and, toward the end of the relationship, abusive Joe became. Rarely was his abuse physical. Most of it was emotional. He would tell her that she was ugly, stupid, no-good, worthless. For a time, she resisted this thinking, remembering how she was cared for, even admired at her last residential care placement and on her job. Gradually, though, after continual emotional battering from Joe, she returned to her original beliefs about herself—that she was no good, and the world would be better off without her.

Her relationship ended with Joe not only leaving her, but "giving" her to one of his friends, who thought even less of her, if possible, than Joe had. She was passed on from man to man, including some work as a prostitute, until she tried to commit suicide. She landed in a hospital bed for two weeks and was in in-patient therapy for three months. Mary came out of the hospital clean and sober, and determined to stay away from men forever. She adopted a dog from the local shelter, moved into her own apartment, and took a job at Goodwill Industries—all with the help of a local social service agency.

Mary was even keel for two years, kind of middle of the road—not allowing herself to feel too down, but not too up either. She was existing. Later, she would say that the only thing that saved her during this period was her dog, who loved her unconditionally, and was always glad to see her when she came home from work.

She lived this way until she met Tom, whom she lives with

today. Tom doesn't abuse her, but he doesn't pay her any special attention either. His job, his life with "the boys" is more important to him than she is. When he's home with Mary he's relatively content and treats her alright, but he soon tires of domestic life and is gone again In short, Tom is with Mary only when he's got nothing else going on. What she wants is irrelevant to him.

In some ways, however, this doesn't bother Mary. She still has her dog and a cat, which are her only constant and faithful companions. And, for now, that seems, ok. She does have a circle of girlfriends that meets almost daily at someone's house. Most of the time they would just sit around and talk and take care of the kids. The backgrounds of these women are similar to her own, as are their present lives. Their husbands or boyfriends do their thing, they come home at night (or they don't) and their lives go on. They don't expect things to get any better and they think they are getting in life just about what they deserve. The little affection and love they have they get from each other, from their children, and from their animals.

But Mary is starting to see herself as different than the other women in her group. She no longer has to fight the urge to self-medicate (the need is no longer there) and is seeing things more clearly--that her friends are blaming others, not themselves for their circumstances. She sees them as stronger than they give themselves credit for being. "I see strengths in them that **they** don't see," she thinks. "Maybe the same is true for me?"

All three of these people are on the verge of major life change.

CHAPTER 4

The nature of human change

There are two kinds of change when it comes to human beings:

1) surface change, or change to the outside only;
2) deep change or growth; change to the inside and outside.

Correspondingly, there are three modes that it is possible for human beings to be operating in at any particular time. They are: survival mode, adjustment mode, and growth mode.

No change takes place when people are in survival mode. Only surface or cosmetic change takes place when people are in the adjustment mode. It is only when people are in the growth mode that substantial change takes place, on the inside and the outside.

Survival mode

While in survival mode, no real change takes place because people don't feel strong enough within themselves to risk leaving the known for the unknown. What they now have may not be ideal, but they know they can tolerate or live with things as they are. You have to understand that change requires one to leave one state of being to enter another state of being. After one has left the first state, there is a transition period before one enters the second state. It could be said that between states, the in-between, one is nothing. It is hard for people with little knowledge of themselves, a low opinion of what they **do** know, and little confidence in their ability to successfully manage their lives to leave the familiar, to tolerate nothingness, and then to adapt to something new and unfamiliar. It is much safer and less anxiety-producing to stay with the familiar, even though the familiar is admittedly bad.

Keep in mind, too, that those in survival mode usually come from a family of individuals who were also in survival mode. Our first lessons are learned by observing our first teachers, our parents and siblings. Furthermore, first lessons are learned when a person is young and with little knowledge of self and the world and, therefore, uncritically accepted as fact. Finally, since taken in while one is so young and helpless, this "knowledge" settles deeply within a person and, after a while, seems to always have been there and to be part of one's being, as is an arm or leg, never to be changed.

Adjustment mode

While in the adjustment mode, people are not as rigidly fixed in their present reality as are those in survival mode. They have had early models of other "adjusters," their parents, and have had lots of practice conforming to the ever-changing norms of attitude and behavior in high school.

Those in the adjustment mode are followers. They look to those outside themselves for their cues as to how to think, behave, and live. They tend to rank themselves as "not as bad as **they** are" when referring to those in survival mode, but "not as good as **they** are," referring to fellow adjusters who more closely resemble, in looks and manners, the current cultural ideal. In their attempt to avoid their greatest fear—standing out from the crowd—they are likely to dress, talk and act like everyone else.

They may openly scorn those in growth mode, because "growers" tend not to pay much attention to cultural trends, but secretly wish they had the "guts" to do so themselves. Typical of adjusters would be hero and celebrity worship. In the extreme, they may be drawn to someone like cult leader, Jim Jones, who led his followers to meaningless deaths in South America.

Growth mode

People in the growth mode, unlike those in the survival or adjustment modes, look inside themselves for their cues as to how to live. Carefully nurtured by their growth- mode parents and siblings, they believe themselves not only good enough and smart enough to chart their own course in life, but also strong enough to stand against those who, mostly out of fear and envy, criticize them. They also feel strong enough to face the uncertainty that what they make of themselves will not be to their liking or to anyone else's.

Like everyone else, growers have within them the instinctual need for affiliation or belonging—that is, to be accepted and loved by others—as well as the need for self- actualization—that is, to become the unique individuals they were born to be. In American society, seeing as how competitive and judgmental it has become, it is difficult to find a balance between these seemingly competing needs. How can one risk answering to his inner voice, rather than the voices of others and society, when he doesn't know if what his inner voice leads him to will be acceptable to other people, whom he realizes he needs? Most people--like adjusters--in the face of this dilemma, tell their inner voice to shut up and merrily join the crowd. But only at a great price, as you will see below.

How does this all relate to the concept of lovable/capable/fit for life? At high school graduation or thereabouts, as stated above, people tend to rate themselves against their peers on attractiveness (lovable) and on smartness (capability). These, together, make up their particular level of self-esteem or perceived adequacy/fitness for life.

If the answer is "no" to the question of "Are you adequate/fit," they either withdraw from reality into insanity, or they die. Survivors answer "yes," as long as they can conceal from themselves their presumably despicable nature. Adjusters answer "yes," as long as they are accepted in "polite" society. Growers answer "yes," as long as they are given the opportunity to explore their own nature and the nature of the world, and act on the answers they develop. From there they make their estimates of what their place is in the world: bottom, middle, top, based on their conceptions of what those mean, generally taken from parents and society (see Exercise 3 below).

In later life—with the benefit of better acquaintance with themselves as they interact with others in their environments--people in all modes generally broaden their conceptions of "lovable," to include inner qualities such as loyalty, common sense, and perceptiveness. And with true life experience and direct knowledge of the world and how it works, they usually broaden their conception of "capable" to include things more than the ability to answer questions on objective tests. With these changes, generally resulting in a better "rating" of themselves against other people in both lovability and capability, as well as a better, more realistic understanding of what constitutes "worthy" ways to occupy their time, people are able to find work that uses them, at least partially, and that provides them with the money to live on as well as pride in their ability to make it on their own.

Nevertheless, people's early programming permits them to go only so far. Survivors will continue to avoid any kind of self-examination for fear of what misfits they fear they'll find themselves to be. They will also stay with the situations, behaviors and people with which they are familiar and they know they can handle.

Again, they did not hear, growing up, that they were inherently good. In fact they usually heard that they were bad, or inferred the same from the actions taken towards them by significant others around them. They don't want to know **how** bad, so don't look. That's why they have to attach themselves to someone else so rigidly for answers to who they are and how to live. In these circumstances, no substantial growth occurs within them from high school on.

Adjusters also continue to look outside themselves for life guidance, but usually to broader society and those who follow its dictates rather than to particular individuals, as do survivors. For them there is a modicum of self examination for personal preferences but, when pressure is applied to comply, they generally buckle and get back in line.

They are not afraid of what they'll see inside—after all, their parents loved them, even though they did not see or treat them as special, and didn't know how to help them counter negative messages. But adjusters are so convinced that stronger/better/smarter others are so much more qualified to answer life questions than they are that they usually accede to the demands of these "superior" people around them. Their prospects for growth, therefore are limited. Some change occurs in this group after high school, but most of it is of a cursory nature.

Growers are the only ones who have the courage to look inside and, despite considerable pressure from other people, perhaps even from parents and close friends, to comply with the "norm," will press on to explore who they are and create a world of their own making from the answers they find. These are people who have no parameters around their feeling, thoughts, and behaviors except for those surrounding the legitimate responsibility they feel towards other people and the society of which they are a part. That being the case they, in small and large ways, have the potential to transform not only themselves, but society itself.

The next three chapters elaborate on the three modes and how Bill, Anne and Mary deal with their unhappiness.

CHAPTER 5

Survival: no change, no adjustment, no growth

For those in survival mode, there is no real change in them—certainly no growth—even as they get older and have direct experience with the world outside high school. They are so busy protecting themselves (even in the absence of the original source of their anxiety) that evidence contrary to their present life stance is not noticed or simply ignored. Without being open to new information that could result in replacing previously held beliefs about themselves and the world with newly-formed beliefs, there can be no growth.

Those in survival mode never get to know who they are or what the world is like because they don't have the luxury of "letting down their guard" long enough to try something new--because it might fail them and that would be devastating.

> Example: I know a 30-year old woman named Julie who had an abusive, alcoholic father when she was growing up who never gave her the love that she needed. Whatever she tried to do for him to get him to love her—wash his clothes, cook his food, drag him home from

the bar at night, get him up in the mornings so he could get to work on time—never worked. He never changed, and she never got from him the love she needed in order for her to love herself. He's dead now, but she still seeks out men who remind her of her father, and bends herself over backwards to earn their love, to no avail. She rejects so-called "decent" men who want to date her because she doesn't know how to act around them. She doesn't know how to respond to men who treat her with respect. She wishes things were different, even that **she** was different. She doesn't like her world, or herself, but she knows she can survive it. Any other world, even a so-called "improvement," she's not sure she could survive. And so, she stays with what she's got. For people like Julie, no matter how old they are, their high school personal and life projections haven't changed a whole lot, nor have their adolescent-like worlds.

Those in survival mode usually come from families in which there was no love at all shown to the children, or it was shown only sporadically and unpredictably. Parents in survival mode usually don't take the time to properly discipline their children--teaching them right from wrong, passing on life lessons from their own experience or learned from their own parents. Parents in survival mode don't consistently support their children as they participate in sports and other extracurricular activities. Parents in survival mode usually don't help their kids with their homework or, for that matter, care how they do in school. Kids from these families, seeing their classmates being treated with love, concern and respect by **their** parents and realizing that they are not, conclude that they are so bad that they are unworthy of anyone's attention or love. After all, if their own parents don't love them, who will?

Often times, there is abuse in these kinds of families—physical, psychological and sexual. Typically, the parents or caregivers are themselves in survival mode and under the influence of mind-altering substances and have nothing positive to give to other people even if they were inclined to do so.

Kids from families such as these become very vigilant. They are very good at judging people's moods because to misjudge, say, their father's mood may mean that, in a drunken rage, he hurts them badly or even kills them. Their wits, therefore, are not used to figure out who they are, but who other people are, because they know that their very survival may depend upon it. Many kids of survivors quickly become addicted to some substance or destructive habits, too, in order to escape, if only for a time, their bleak existence.

Not surprisingly, these kids usually deem themselves at high school graduation (if they make it that far), unlovable and incapable of dealing with the world on their own. They usually predict for themselves only a marginal future. Their reading of themselves usually doesn't change over the years, unless something intervenes that allows them to see themselves as something other than losers.

Mary

Mary came from a home in survival mode. Her mother was in survival mode when Mary was a child. She tried to love her child, but was so overcome with her own survival needs that she didn't have the strength, in the end, to even take care of Mary's physical needs, much less her emotional ones. Mary interpreted her removal from her mother's home as being that her mother didn't love her or want her—therefore, she must be very, very bad. She carried that feeling with her for years. During this period, she was in survival mode, attaching herself to any man who showed any interest in being with her or taking care of her, without any thought that there were different kinds of men--some good for her, some bad. She lived to please whomever she was with. She learned to read her partners' moods so as not to upset them and risk getting beat up, or worse.

Over the years and with different men, she became pregnant two times, both of which ended in abortion, because the men didn't want the children, but also because something in her told her that she was not fit to raise a child right then, just as her mother had not been. She bore the pain of losing her first two babies but, not wanting to go through that again, she got on birth control pills.

It was in residential treatment that Mary's inherent good nature was nurtured and she began to think that life did not have to be for her what it was and as it had been for her mother. She was told and started to believe that there was decency in her and that she was appreciated. She haltingly started down the growth path, until she met Joe, causing her to fall back into survival mode.

CHAPTER 6

Adjustment: change, but external only

Those in adjustment mode, the vast majority of Americans, do change but for the most part, only peripherally. Their parents gave them love, but were not able to act as the buffer that they needed when confronted by a judgmental society at a very crucial time in their lives, when kids are making judgments about themselves and their future based on high school comparisons.

Parents don't know about, or don't know how to help their kids deal with, the pressures to be a certain way in high school, and the tendency of kids to rank themselves in comparison to their classmates on such things as looks and smarts. When their kid comes home from school, having been bullied, they are likely to say, with great compassion, something like: "That's all right, honey; we love you." It is important for the kid to know that his parents are behind him, but he also knows that he has to go back to school the next day and probably be bullied again. His parents may call the principal and fight for him, but they don't know how devastating criticism is at this age, how vulnerable their kid is to unfair comparisons, don't know how to combat it, and don't realize, themselves, how precious their kid is, not having been valued as such by their **own** parents, in their time

The effect of all this is that most kids are on their own. Parents care but don't know how to help. Their attitude is something like: "We made it through school; they will too." If their kids end up feeling special (a key ingredient to those who eventually make it to the growth mode), it is usually not the parent who starts them down that road; rather, it's a relative who sees something of value, a teacher who recognizes herself in her, a coach who helps him discover and develop a latent talent.

Kids, left on their own, are likely to judge themselves by society's standards rather than by internal ones. Am I lovable becomes, "Am I good-looking." Am I capable becomes, "can I do enough so as not to seem 'different' than other people." Fitting in becomes the mantra. In later life, they end up playing a grown-up version of the "please love me" game they played as children.

> Example: had Julie, the woman who was in survival mode and who endured for years the abuse of her boyfriend, been in adjustment mode instead, she would probably have tolerated the abuse for a time, if the abuser was viewed by others as good-looking, or cool, or influential. Eventually, however, she would have found the relationship not worth the trouble and moved on. I have seen cases, however, where the woman (or the man) stays. If so, the constant degrading of the person usually results in her falling into survival mode.

Anne

Anne's parents were in the growth mode when she was growing up and encouraged the same in their children, with a twist. They were all told that they were loved, but it was clear to all that the boys were favored in the family. It was the boys who could do anything or be anything, while the girls were expected to take up their prescribed roles as helpmates to their husbands and good wives and mothers with the attendant duties flowing there from. Furthermore, whether from lack of time or understanding, the girls were never told who would make a good husband and provider and what went into making a good marriage.

In this atmosphere and into her adult life, Anne carried the notion that her parents loved her and that she was valuable, but only as their child and as a wife and mother. When she made noises about college she was discouraged because it was frivolous, off purpose. When she told of her dreams of being a doctor, she was not taken seriously. It was something that would pass when she realized the futility of it. She knew that if either of the boys had entertained such a career notion, it would have been encouraged by her parents, because a man's role was to make a good living for his family.

The upshot of all this for Anne was that she was supposed to dabble in jobs until someone came along and married/rescued her, at which time her real life would start as helpmate, wife and mother. She abandoned her dreams of a medical career and self-sufficiency and, with no notion other than what her parents had modeled and what she had heard from her girlfriends concerning what a good marriage was, stepped into life. She had no real reason to look into herself for her answers—her parents had given her all the answers she needed. She need only wait. Anne was, therefore, in an adjustment/ growth mode—looking to her parents for answers and a man to come along and approve of her, yet sensing that there was something in her that was better than that.

CHAPTER 7

Growth: change, internal & external

Those in growth mode were usually loved and treated as if they were special from the time they were born. Those who regard themselves as special don't look to others for advice as to how to act. They come to appreciate their own internal voices as the only reliable guide to their actions. Their parents treat them as if they are as good on the inside as they are on the outside, and they transmit this truth to their kid in many ways.

This is not to say that "growth" kids are pampered. When they do wrong, they are told so, but in such a way that they learn from the experience, rather than shamed by it. Growth parents are just as intent on teaching their kids the proper restraints that society places on individual behavior as they are in fostering the individual growth of their kids. After all, they realize that their kids will have to create their lives within the context of society.

Parents of "growers" are aware that all kids are special, deep down, but that most don't find this out. They are aware of the instinctual need that human beings have to belong, but also of our instinctual need to grow, to actualize in our lives who we are and have been since birth. They see their kids as a gift to the world who need to be made aware of their goodness on the inside and outside, and of the unlimited future that awaits them.

They realize that the brains of their children were designed to enable them to figure out who they are and how to best use that discovered self in the world. This is in contrast to those in the other modes who are taught, directly or indirectly, that others know better than they do how they should live their lives.

Kids who are convinced that they are "ok," as they are, do not become slaves to other people or to society's dictates. They are able to look inward for guidance, and are allowed latitude by their growth-mode parents to grow as their own nature dictates. They feel the pressure of society, but do not succumb to it because they know that would mean turning their backs on themselves and their own ideas about who they are, what the world is like and their place in it.

In school, they are not grade slaves—that is, they can feel good about themselves whether they earn "C's" or "A's." They are friends to everyone, not just the "cool" group. In looking for friends, they look to the inside of people, not just to their outside, or their fidelity to current fashion.

They consider themselves lovable, even if some other people say otherwise. As to capable, they realize that they have gifts and have them to use in the world for the good of themselves and others. They are confident that they will be able to create a life that will draw from them that which they are uniquely able to give. Not only do they consider themselves fit for life, they believe that life as they know it can be made a little bit better, due to their own actions.

Growers are capable of deep, profound change, but don't pursue change for change's sake. They look forward to their own development, knowing that their lives will constantly change, as their understanding of themselves and of the world changes. Their allegiance is not to society, but to themselves and their constant pursuit of the truth about who they are and what they are here on earth to do.

> Example: had Julie been in growth mode, she wouldn't have tolerated at all an abusive partner, saying to herself something like: "Who is this person to think he can treat me with disrespect?"

Bill

Bill's parents were in growth mode when he was growing up and, therefore, could and did appreciate him for who he was and wanted him to grow into who he could become. They assumed that who he was, deep down, was good and pure and the only rational basis upon which Bill could build his life. So they praised and loved him for who he was, just as he was, and also for what he could become in the future.

Bill was a spirited youngster and got into his share of trouble. As a boy, he stole a toy from a downtown store. His parents made him take the toy back and apologize to the manager. One summer he was caught with a bunch of other boys "raiding" gardens. Again, his parents sent him to apologize. He was caught cheating on a math test in ninth grade. His parents grounded him for two weeks for this incident and used it to teach Bill about honesty and hard work. He was often in the principal's office, usually for "cutting up" in class. As he got older, there were some drinking incidents and he put a few dents in the family car. There was a period, too, when he developed the habit of lying to his parents. Exasperated as they were by these incidents, Bill's parents used them to teach Bill about the balance we must all find between personal freedom and our responsibility to ourselves, and our responsibility to other people and to society.

Throughout all this, however, they encouraged Bill to listen to and act upon the silent urgings of his inner voice, telling him what was right for him to do while, of course, taking into account the responsibilities he had to other people and to society. They celebrated his victories with him and stood behind him as he learned from his setbacks—not defeats, but opportunities to refine his knowledge of who he was and how the world worked.

As he grew older, and the consequences of his actions became more and more predictable and positive for him, and he became more confident in himself and his decision-making ability, Bill's parents gave him (based on their estimation of his ability to handle any "bad" consequences his behaviors might bring) increasing latitude to act on his own behalf. As a result, Bill's confidence in himself and his ability to create happiness in his life steadily increased.

They knew about Bill what they had already learned about themselves and about the world: that people are inherently good and that they are made the way they are for a reason. They knew that people were made as they are because they each have a particular role to play in life, and that the clues to what one's role is is found in his interests, his predilections, and his personal likes and dislikes. They told Bill that who he was was beautiful and that his mission in life would be revealed to him to the extent that he accepted himself as he was, and the world as it is.

They also knew that Bill would encounter the "outside" world as he went through school and matured. They knew that Bill would hear the siren song from other people and from society that would whisper to him who he was and what he should do and be.

They also knew that from within Bill himself would come not only the need to be who he was, but also the need to belong. They knew that he would eventually realize that he had to live the bulk of his life amongst his peers, not amongst his family, and that human beings had a powerful need to belong to their peer group, a peer group that for the most part follows society's dictates, dictates that would likely clash with the urgings of his inner voice. They tried to make him realize that he didn't need everyone to like him, only a few, and for the right reasons—because they appreciated him, just the way he was.

However desirable it may seem to be in growth mode, however, it is not without its problems, as you will presently see.

CHAPTER 8

The courage to change

Growth, especially major growth, doesn't come easily. Even people in growth mode have a way of being that they've worked hard to achieve, that integrates all they know about themselves and the world into a coherent whole, and with which they are intimately familiar and comfortable. Such a way of being allows them to face life with confidence and anticipation.

Any new information that has the potential to overturn this hard-won structure is, for a time, resisted. Resisted, that is, not rejected as is true in the case of those in the other two modes. The new information tends to be set aside until one is strong enough to let it in and then ridden like a bronco to wherever it takes him—that is, until it all comes together again into a coherent whole. And usually at a higher level of consonance with reality. This is growth toward maturity.

Growth of this kind requires a personality structure that is flexible enough to accommodate change and a person confident enough to believe that the change, even though he doesn't know where it will lead, will leave him stronger and better than before.

Growth of this kind in individuals is the only thing that makes for real change in the world—that is, strong individuals listening to their inner voices and following their unique passions.

What was the impetus for change, the new information encountered, for our 3 people? Read on:

Bill's turning point

One day, while working with a man who had bad headaches that he thought might be related to a previous neck injury, Bill began to suspect that the pain was more in the man's psyche than in his body. He referred him to the resident psychiatrist and the man was cured. But, unlike other cases, Bill dwelled on this one. "How does psychic pain relate to physical pain," he asked himself. "How does all this relate to other people I know? How does this relate to me and my problems?" While kicking this all around in his head, something remarkable began to happen—for some reason, he started feeling alive again, and excited and hopeful for the first time in years. But in the middle of this euphoria was the image of his father, who seemed to be showing up in his dreams more often—usually gazing at him disapprovingly, while shaking his head.

Now Bill was one who was told for as long as he could remember that he was loveable and loved, and that he was capable of dealing with what life presented him. He was told, indeed, that he could make of his life what he wanted to. He realized that he was capable of analyzing himself and the world and coming up with solutions that would make things better for him, that would give him reason for optimism and hope. After all, had he not been able to do so up to this difficult period in his life?

As time went on, it became increasingly clear to him that he was still interested in working with people who were in pain, but not physical pain, psychic pain—with people struggling with their lives, trying to find meaning in them in a seemingly meaningless world. He realized that he, too, was looking for meaning in his life. What could he do with himself that really made sense to him, that was his reason for being?

He had a clue in his seemingly inordinate and continuing interest in the patient he had who had physical symptoms but with psychological origins. As he continued to review his life and the decisions that he had made to get to where he was, he recalled his college interests in religion and psychology. He remembered his old professor who had so inspired him in his undergraduate years. On a whim, one day, he decided to look up his old professor, Dr. Wilhelm. He called the school, found out that he had recently retired and that he still lived in town. He found his number in the phone book and called.

When he met with Dr. Wilhelm and explained to him what was going on with him, it was as if a floodgate had been opened in him. He talked non-stop for two hours. Most of the content of his talk was of his growing excitement about people—their spiritual selves, not just their physical selves, their souls, not just their bodies. When he stopped talking, Dr. Wilhelm said: "It sounds to me as if you know what you want to do. What's stopping you from doing it?" Bill said "Two things--one: I'm contemplating getting out of medicine altogether, and that would mean a real change for me and a downgrading of my lifestyle, with implications for my family, all of whom have become accustomed to the way things are now and, two: I keep thinking that I am letting down my father, and that stops me every time."

"What is it that you are thinking about, if not psychiatry," asked Dr. Wilhelm.

"I'm thinking about the ministry," Bill said, "divinity school, and a life as a preacher. It's the soul I'm interested in. Why are we here? Where are we going? How can I help people on their earthly journey? I know it sounds foolish. But it's what keeps coming to my mind."

"You know your mind and your heart, Bill; listen to them," said Dr Wilhelm.

"But what of my father, Dr." Bill replied." I'd be letting him down. In my heart I know that it would be hard for my family to adjust to the change, but I believe they could do it, but I just don't know about my father."

"Would he want you to be happy, Bill," Dr. Wilhelm asked.

After some thought, Bill replied, "Yes, he would. I have no doubt that he wanted the best for me."

"What would he say to you if he were alive and in this room right now," asked Dr. Wilhelm. Bill got out of his chair and paced awhile before he stopped and said, "I think he would tell me to follow my heart, just as he followed his to medicine. He would say he didn't want to be the cause of my unhappiness." The room was silent for a long time after he said this. A feeling of peace came over Bill that he had not known for a long time. He also did something else he had not done in years--he cried. But these were not tears of grief, but tears of relief--relief at having found his way.

Within the next five years, Bill completely transformed his life. He left medicine and entered the seminary. He is now an ordained minister. He repaired his marriage and his relationship with his kids. They sold their house and cars, moved to a neighborhood close to the church and, after a period of adjustment, are all much closer and happier now.

Questions of lovability and capability and fitness for life are no longer of concern to Bill. He is where he belongs and he knows it. He is not comparing himself to others; he is living on purpose and even with a sense of mission. He has transcended other people's opinions of him and is creating a life full of meaning for himself. He feels that his ministry is what he was born to do—it draws on his essence, asks of him what he wants and needs to give to the world, and affords him the feeling that he is "home."

Anne's turning point

What turned Anne around was two-fold: 1) at work, a few of her co-workers encouraged her to go for an open supervisor's job, saying that if he (the previous supervisor) could do it, she could do it—she agreed; 2) her increasing self-confidence in managing her and her daughter's life, on her own.

Working in the paint department for nine months or so, and liking it better than any department she had been in previously, she found that she knew the business, knew paint, knew what to ask customers, and knew how to help them. Increasingly, customers were specifically seeking her out for help. In fact, her supervisor too was frequently coming to her for help in his job. When he resigned, co-workers as well as a couple managers from other departments encouraged her to go for the job.

Anne was flattered, and she seriously considered the move for awhile. Eventually, however, she decided that manager of a department store was not what she wanted to be. She wanted to be a nurse. So she quit and went back to school, where she is now. Every day she is feeling more comfortable with her choice, more confident that she is now on the way to her true vocation.

One of the big reasons she went for nursing, also, was because of her daughter. She knew that her daughter was watching her and she wanted to model for her competence, happiness in her work and, of course, self-sufficiency. Furthermore, nursing would eventually pay more than her previous work, call for more of her competence, and looked as though it was a growing field.

After awhile Anne's parents even started seeing her differently, as more competent and independent.

Like Bill, Anne feels, for the first time, that she is doing something that just seems "right." Her schooling is drawing from the deepest parts of her, the part that she is coming to believe she was born to give.

Mary's turning point

Mary has gradually come to the belief that she wants to get married and to have a baby that both her future husband and herself will raise. In participating in and listening to the discussions with the other women in her group (and remembering lessons learned in residential care) she is coming to believe that the source of her problems, and the major barrier to the life she dreams of, is a faulty self-appraisal. Her life experience had, to this point, led her to believe that she was a bad person and she acted in ways consonant with that belief. She only deserved in life what a bad person deserved.

As the months and years in the women's group went on, however, she began to diverge from the group and gradually came to believe that she wasn't a bad person and that she deserved something better; that she deserved a good life and didn't have to settle for what she had. The thought came into her mind to start over—to end her "relationship" with Tom, to move out of her apartment, quit her job, move to a place where no-one knew her, and begin again. She was biding her time, mustering her courage, to do just that.

She now works in a group home, much like the ones she was in as a kid. She is much admired and loved by staff and child alike because everyone knows she understands and cares. Her previous life makes sense to her now, as she believes that, as painful as it was, it was in preparation for what she does now and which draws from her what she is and what she has to give.

She lives in her own place now with her dog and three cats. She is in a committed relationship with a man who has a young daughter, who loves her, respects her, and shares her goals for a larger family and a stable life.

PART 2

How about you?

Alternative One: to be read by those who don't have What's Your Story and What's Your Career. For those who do have these two tools, skip to Alternative Two, starting on page 89.

CHAPTER 9

Comparisons

What do these three people have to do with you and your life? After all, you are grown-up, respected, and successful. Well, all I can say to you is that however "grown-up" you are, there lives within you the child you were. Furthermore, some of the childhood decisions you made about who you were and what was possible for you also still live in you and affect you today.

Do you doubt me? Have you ever gone "home" to your parent's house for the holidays and found yourself acting like the child or sibling you once were? Have you ever attended a high school reunion and observed yourself, and your classmates, revert to the roles you all played when you were in high school? Have you ever found yourself suddenly transported to a previous time in your life at an unsuspected sound, sight, or smell?

I like the story of the young husband who, after a Sunday meal of roast ham, idly asked his wife why she always cut the ends off her ham roasts. The wife replied that that was the way her mother always did it. Curious now herself, she called her mother and asked her why she always cut her ham in this way. Her reply: because her pan was too small to do otherwise! Another example of automatic action, from the past, without conscious thought. How many of our actions have similar origins—automatic, unconscious, from the past and, like the ham story, off the mark? Keep in mind that conclusions drawn and beliefs set, **no matter when formed**, usually stay alive and active unless re-examined and changed in light of present reality.

Since beliefs drive behaviors, if your beliefs are faulty, your behaviors will also be faulty—that is, your decisions will be based on false information, leading to unanticipated, probably unwanted consequences. Keep in mind that most people tend to forget their past as they grow up, not knowing that decisions made then about who they are and what they can become, affect them today. If they are not happy as adults, chances are the source of their unhappiness is trying to live in the present based on faulty conceptualizations from the past.

That's what therapy is all about: going back in time, looking at old beliefs formed at a time when you were a dependent child who had little facility to judge the accuracy of the information you were taking in from your environment. Unless those beliefs have been revisited in adulthood, chances are good that they still live in you today. In therapy one looks, with an adult mind, at faulty beliefs formed in childhood with the aim of replacing them with beliefs that conform to one's present, adult reality.

I've also found that "success" in this country is a slippery concept. I have encountered many people who, by all outward appearances—power, prestige, money, possessions, etc.—are what most people and society would call successful, but deem themselves unhappy and discontent. Imagine struggling mightily for and finally possessing all that the world has to offer and finding, in the end, not happiness but instead that "is this all there is" feeling. If you have everything that society holds dear and it does not make you happy, does that mean there is something wrong with society, or with you? Where does one go from there?

Are you successful? Maybe the better question is, are you happy? Most people answer this question with something like: "Well, I'm not unhappy, but I can't say I'm happy either." Many of us are familiar with the "is this all there is" feeling, suspecting that there is "something more" for us out there, but don't know where to find it. The more contemplative of us realize that the "more" is not to be found by looking outside ourselves into the world but inward, within ourselves. So let's take an inward look.

Let's begin by taking a reading of your **present** life perspective. Keeping in mind the definitions provided previously in this book, complete these exercises as best you can, from your present point of view:

Exercise 1

Am I <u>lovable</u>: evidence for this.

+ = <u>Adequate/Fit for life</u>

Am I <u>capable</u>: evidence for this.

At what level are you adequate/fit for life? Explain:

1) adequate, a creator of my own life (Grower)
2) adequate, an efficient follower (Adjuster)
3) adequate, as long as nothing changes (Survivor)

Based on your answers to Exercise 1, answer the 3 vital life questions:

Exercise 2

Who am I?

What's the world like?

What's my place in the world?

Exercise 3

Where would you place yourself on the following scales?

Attractiveness	Intelligence	Careers
Brad Pitt/ Angelina Jolie	Albert Einstein/ Margaret Thatcher	Doctor/lawyer
|	|	|
|	|	|
|	|	|
|	|	|
|	|	|
|	|	|
|	|	|
|	|	|
|	|	|
Ernest Borgnine/ Ruth Buzzi	Three stooges/ Edith Bunker	Hamburger flipper

Now, I'd like to help you recreate, as closely as possible, your world in the year of your high school graduation. Three dimensions are important in this endeavor: your home, your school, and your home town or city.

Home

First, you'll need to find pictures and/or objects that can represent your parents and your siblings, plus any other people (grandparents, cousins, or other relatives) or pets that were important to you at that time in your life. It would also be helpful to find pictures of your home, inside and outside, as well as the neighborhood in which it was located. Make sure you include a picture of yourself at that time that you feel represents the real "you," which best personifies the thoughts and feelings you had about yourself and the world at that vital period in your life. Include any objects or artifacts that remind you of that family, that kid, and that time.

School

Next, locate pictures and artifacts that will allow you to represent your school, your classmates, and your teachers and good friends or chums who were around you and important to you as you were about to graduate from high school. Yearbooks are helpful here, as are signed copies of your yearbook pictures. Again, objects that will help transport your mind back to that time--an old letter jacket, the program from the senior prom, saved articles from the local paper—will be helpful.

Town/City

Finally, find some pictures and/or objects that will remind you of the town/city you grew up in and the school you attended when you were a teenager. If you don't have any tangible artifacts of your old hangouts and other places in town where you spent significant time, find a soft chair in a quiet spot and drift back in time to a day or week that is particularly memorable and re-live it in your mind, using all your senses to help you make the past present.

Next, on a table with lots of room and in a way that makes sense to you, arrange all these artifacts around the picture you chose to represent yourself. Focus on that picture. Allow yourself to see and know that person you were (and, in some ways, still are) in that picture. Allow yourself to go back in time and inhabit that person you were then. In your mind, surround yourself with the people, things, and the environment from back then. Place yourself in the location that was most vivid in you memory as you did the "re-living" exercise above.

Breathe life into the scene. Zero in on your young self in that special place and time; think what you were thinking then, feel what you were feeling then, dream as you did then. Use any other objects, people or stratagems that will allow you to conjure up the world you lived in then and how you felt about yourself and about life in it. Are you there? Good. Now, from the point of view of this young person, do exercises 1, 2, and 3 again.

Most people find quite a difference in their responses to the exercises when answered as the adults they are as opposed to those of the adolescents they were. Why? Because, in the years since high school graduation, they have tested what were merely predictions or assumptions about what **might** happen against reality—what actually **did** happen to them. What proved to be demonstrably false in their early predictions was replaced by reality.

What did you find? If you are like most people, you will have discovered a variation of: "I feel more comfortable in my own skin. I'm less hard on myself for my 'failures.' I'm more confident that I can 'make it' financially and otherwise in the world, despite frequent changes in the world and the workplace." But, I also hear this: "Despite all this, I'm not as happy as I had hoped to be at this point in my life."

It is my guess that **you** are not as happy as you hoped to be at this point in your life, that what you have gained in understanding about yourself and the world over the years is not enough for you. How do I know this? Because you are reading this book. If you were satisfied with your life as it is, you wouldn't be reading about discovering the person you were "meant to be"; you would be out happily living your life. I surmise that you are experiencing a variation of the "is this all there is" syndrome suffered by the "successful" people described above. If it makes you feel any better, you are not alone. There are a whole lot of people out there, just like you, thinking the same thing but afraid to admit it.

Why? You've worked hard, played the game. Where are the promised rewards in happiness and contentment for a life lived doing what you were supposed to do? Could it be that what you have learned over the years--that has admittedly improved your life, although leaving you wishing for more—constitutes only cosmetic improvements? That is, from high school graduation to now did you merely refine your "moves," learn to play society's game better? Did you get better at adjusting to and accommodating society, but still feel unfulfilled? What if what you're doing now with your "career" and "lifestyle" is merely playing a more sophisticated version of the "please love me" game you played in high school with your classmates? Are you saying to yourself, "there's got to be more than this?"

The good news is that there is, indeed, more than this. But it takes hard work to find it. And "it" is not to be found **outside** of you, in society, but **inside** you. And the search begins where it started: in your past.

It has been my professional experience that, in order to grow, one must first remove blocks to growth: faulty conclusions from one's past and beliefs about oneself and the world that are untrue.

Let's start with a closer look at your birth family.

CHAPTER 10

Home

Set aside for a time the school and town/city artifacts you chose for the previous reading and let's focus on the remaining "home" artifacts. Perhaps you have remembered important objects or pictures that weren't a part of your first "reading" — add them. Include in the scene some old "stair step" pictures of yourself from kindergarten or thereabouts to the picture you chose in the first reading that encapsulated "you" as a late adolescent so as to give you a sense of your total, conscious experience in this family. Add what you need of old family pictures and objects to give the picture body. Make sure you include a Christmas picture where everyone is included and there is a favorite, characteristic pose in it by you.

Finally, arrange the whole in a way that makes sense to you.

Now, immerse yourself in the scene. Let yourself, first, remember how it was and then, give it the spark of life and live it again, as best you can. (It helps some people to do this in the company of a trusted friend; the friend can best help by just listening to you, without comment, unless told otherwise).

Focus first on your parents or primary care-givers. Were they in the survival mode adjustment mode or the growth mode, as described above? How did this fact manifest itself in your family?

Now, focus on dad. What was he like then? Describe him in a few words. How would you answer this: "Dad would always say_____." What was his general outlook on life? What was his relationship with your mother? How did he view, treat her? How did he view and treat women in general? Men in general? How did he view, treat his kids? How did he view, treat you?

Do the same with your mother. How did your parents get along, treat one another? How did they parent? Did they set your feet on the path of the growth mode, adjustment mode, or survival mode?

From the scene, choose a favorite family picture—perhaps the Christmas picture. Are these people happy or sad? Why or why not? In the picture, are you happy or sad? Why?

Now choose separate pictures for all your family members. Go over them individually. Tell your friend about all of them, then and now. Where were you in the birth order? How did this affect you? What roles did each take in the family? What was your role? Do you still play that role today, in your family and otherwise?

Finally, choose from the scene a favorite picture of yourself. Tell your friend all about this kid as if the kid was a good friend, rather than yourself: "This is <u>your name</u>. She is ...." What are your feelings towards this kid? Was he/she good/bad, lovable/unlovable, capable/incapable, worthy of love and caring/unworthy of loving and caring? Explain.

Did you feel loved by dad, by mom, by your siblings? Did you feel that your family treated you with respect? Explain.

After you are deeply into your feelings about yourself and

your family at this time in your life, ask yourself the following questions:

- If you felt disrespected or mistreated by your father, did you conclude (with your child mind), that you were unworthy of respect?
- If you felt second-best in comparison to your siblings in the eyes of your mother, did your conclude (with your child mind) that your were unlovable?
- If your family was too large for your parents to give you the individual attention you needed, did you conclude (with your child mind) that you were insignificant?
- If your oldest sister was the "beauty queen" of the school, did you (with your child mind) conclude that you were ugly?
- If your older brother, whom you considered your best friend, went off to college and "forgot" you, did you conclude (with your child mind) that you were forgettable?
- If your mother and father split up when you were a child, did you conclude (with your child mind), that it was your fault?
- If you were put up for adoption because your parent/parents couldn't/wouldn't take care of you, did you conclude (with your child mind), that there was something wrong with you and no-one would want you?
- If your father wanted you to fulfill a dream in the world that he couldn't, did you (with your child mind) conclude that you had to do it for him, or you wouldn't be a "good" son?
- If your parents believed that boys were more "valuable" than girls, and you're a girl, did you conclude (with your

child mind), that all boys were more valuable than you were?

- Add any others that came to you as you were time-traveling in the "previous time" exercise above and/or that occur to you now:

If ……………………, did you conclude (with your child mind) that…………………?

These, and uncountable other false, yet limiting beliefs are what cause us to think less of ourselves than we are, and constrict our dreams. While feeling the hurt that still exists from these old, yet familiar beliefs, stand up to them and, with your adult mind, dispute the truth of them. For example: Isn't it true--and you can see it clearly now that you are an adult—that your father had no respect to give to you because he didn't respect himself? Your resulting belief--a belief that is as true for you today as it was then--that you are unworthy of respect, is incorrect. So what is correct? Are you worthy of respect? Why? You may, now, also have to reevaluate how you feel about your father. He may no longer be, in your mind, the personification of evil (or virtue) you always thought he was—but, on the other hand, he'll probably be more human to you. And your self-respect will rise. Chances are too that, after a time, your relationship with him will improve.

In this simulation, what did you learn about yourself, life and where you might fit in life? Share these feelings and thoughts with your friend. Acknowledge and make friends with the vulnerable, yet precious child that still lives in you today.

How did what you concluded about yourself and the world when you were a vulnerable and dependent child affect how you answered the lovable/capable questions above? What burdens from your past do you carry to this day? Are there things of value that you've always had, but forgotten about that you need to recover and use? Are there things that you carry that are no longer true or useful (if they ever were) that you want to let go?

CHAPTER 11

School and other people

I have found that, like one's birth family, one's K-12 schooling has a great impact on how a person feels about himself and his future prospects in the world. Family is understandable, as demonstrated in Chapter 11. What is it, though, about early schooling?

I believe one's first school experience is so impactful because it's a person's initiation into the outer world, where one encounters ideas and ways of being that are different from what one has learned at home. I think, too, it's important because one realizes that it is in this setting, without the protection of one's family and in the company of these strange "others" that the bulk of one's life will be lived and one must sink or swim with them.

It is the first setting in which one has to choose whom to believe--parents or peers and the popular culture with which they are imbued. Furthermore, people outside one's family don't **have** to love you because you are "family." "Outsiders," therefore, will love you or not based on your merits, or lack thereof. Finally, it's at school that kids are, in effect, ranked according to their grades. Many kids with a 2.0 grade-point average in school resign themselves to a 2.0 future.

Throw in the strong feelings and emotions associated with physical maturing and you have the ingredients of a strong brew, boiling away. Balancing these powerful influencers, some of which undoubtedly sending opposite messages, one takes his first tentative steps toward a personal philosophy. That is why conclusions drawn, and beliefs established at this tumultuous time of life tend to set one's mode of feeling, thinking, and acting that, unless seriously challenged in some way—be it chance events, natural maturing, or therapy—will remain throughout one's life.

Set aside the "home" pictures and artifacts for the time being and retrieve the ones you chose to represent "school." Scan your collection of memorabilia for any images or artifacts that whisper "school" to you, even your earliest days in school if they seem important to you—add them. Complete the scene with any pictures, yearbooks, or mementos that can help you get in the mood to go back in time. I recommend that you have a close friend, perhaps even an old classmate, with you as you reminisce, and with whom you can share old triumphs and hurts. Some people find it useful, prior to this session, to visit their old school. Arrange the pictures and accessories in a way that makes sense to you.

Begin with a favorite picture of yourself in a school setting around graduation time, one that personifies what you thought about yourself and about life in general at this time in your life. Perhaps it's the same one you used previously. What about this kid? What is he/she wearing? What is the setting? What is he/she thinking/feeling in this picture? How does he/she compare to his/her classmates? Tell this all to your trusted friend. In detail, describe this kid, yourself, to your friend as if the kid was someone close that you used to know very well. Now, immerse yourself in this young person and his/her world, as you did with your family above. Once "there," ask:

- If your best friend moved away before you graduated and you never saw or heard from him/her again, did you conclude (with your child mind) that it hurts too badly to get too close to people?
- If you were a bone-head in math, did you conclude (with your child mind) that you were stupid?
- If you were always chosen last for games in PE class, did you conclude (with your child mind) that you were not physically competitive and would have to rely on your brain alone to get along in the world? No marathons for you?
- If you were targeted by a bully who told you that you were fat and ugly, did you conclude (with your child mind) that you were, indeed, fat and ugly and therefore bad?
- If you were dating a variety of boys to see what kind of boys there were out there and, consequently, were told by some that you were a "slut," did you conclude (with your child mind) that you were, indeed, a slut?
- If you slept with a lot of girls in high school and your buddies, in consequence, called you a "stud," did you conclude (with your child mind) that you were, indeed, a stud?
- If you were "smarter" than most of your classmates, did you conclude (with your child mind) that you were better than they were, too?
- If you were intimately acquainted with the principal's of-

fice, did you conclude (with your child mind) that you were "one bad dude."

- If you fell in love with one of your teachers and she married another man, did you conclude (with your child mind), that you would never love another woman? (I did that. It turned out not to be true!)

- Add others relevant to your situation:

If ...., did you conclude (with your child mind) that............

Again, feel the hurt, and then express the hurt to your friend (whom you've instructed to just listen, no matter what you say or do—unless asked to do differently). With your adult mind, dispute the truth of your early conclusions. With the bullying example above, realize that the bully was a troubled kid; he probably thought that **he** was ugly and was trying to deal with the pain of this by attacking you.

Again, looking at a picture of yourself taken at that time, ask yourself, as if looking at someone other than yourself: "Is this kid fat and ugly?" And, "Do I consider myself fat and ugly, now?" And, finally: "Have I held myself hostage to this boy all these years?"

Consider the impact of holding such a belief might have had, and continues to have, on your self-esteem, your perceived fitness for life and subsequent life choices.

CHAPTER 12

Society

Society, or one's culture, is so big, so ever-present, so insistent that it is hard to resist its dictates. And dictate it does. Through advertisements, companies want to convince you that you will not fit or belong with your contemporaries if you do not buy their products. Movies and magazines present to us the "ideal" male and female in looks, attitudes, and behaviors. Once indoctrinated with its dictates, "citizens" like us tend to re-indoctrinate one another until it seems that the only way to avoid being an outcast is to conform to society's ever-changing demands. And it is in this environment that we know, even at age 18, that we must prepare ourselves for careers and for marriage and families.

Set aside your school materials and retrieve the ones you chose to represent your town or city. Let them represent for you the world or life as you knew it as an 18-year-old. Make sure you include in the mix the picture you originally chose to represent yourself. You might have stored away pictures of you with your best friend/friends at this vital time in your life—add them. It might help to visit your old home town and, perhaps, answer some of these questions with a group of old classmates. Again, pictures and artifacts have a way of helping people take themselves back in time so they are not just reminiscing, but actually re-living earlier times. Find some that remind you of the times you lived as a budding adolescent. Some people find it helpful to add to the mix pictures from magazines that were popular in those days. When you are "in character," answer the following:

- If you saw most of the people around you smoking, did you conclude (with your child mind) that you must smoke, too, in order to not be excluded?
- Did you conclude (with your child mind) that those people who most closely resembled the "teen idols" of the time, were better than those who didn't, like yourself?
- If your grades were just "ok" in high school, did you conclude (with your child mind) that you could only hope for an "ok" kind of job and life?
- If your family could not afford the clothes and accessories that most other kids were wearing in school, did you conclude (with your child mind) that they were better than you?
- When you observed that towns-people with white-collar occupations seemed to have more money and prestige than those with blue-collar occupations, did you (with your child mind) conclude that white-collar people are better than blue collar people?
- Did you conclude (with your child mind) that children of white-collar parents were better than the children of blue-collar parents?
- Add other scenarios relevant to your situation:

If……………………………….., did you conclude (with your child mind) that ……………..

Again, allow yourself to feel the hurt that may arise in you as a result of this exercise. Express your hurt to your friend or friends. Now, consider with your adult mind, whether or not any of it is true. More importantly, whether objectively true or not, did you believe it to be true, and live as if it were true? Do you today?

Consider the impact on your present life of holding untruths, as truths. Remember, society or other people can only hurt you if you believe the nasty things they are saying to you, about you. As a child, you may have felt that you had no choice but to believe; as an adult, you do.

Do you feel better? Lighter? Freer? Have you realized, yet, that your negative thoughts about yourself were the result of your own faulty conclusions, based on child-like reasoning? Have you realized that the greatest barrier to a better, more meaningful life for yourself has been, and remains, yourself? Do you realize that you do not have to compare yourself to other people and that the only meaningful, useful comparison to be made is between who you are now and who you could be? Do you realize that no court in the land is going to prosecute you if you choose to live a life of your own choosing, one that is different than that of most others? Do you realize that you are not a freak of nature, less than other people, boring, insignificant, unworthy of the good things in life? Do you realize that you are the way you are for a reason?

Do you realize that you are okay, just the way you are if you'll but **be** who you are?

CHAPTER 13

Take your pick

What you have done to this point, is purge yourself of what you are not. You have started thinking for yourself rather than passively accepting what other people and your culture say you are and/or should be. What this means for you is that you have recovered the power of choice. Other people or entities no longer have the power to make your choices for you, unless you consciously let them do so. So what will you do with this new freedom? What will you choose: the easy route of passively following society's dictates, or the much more difficult, but infinitely more gratifying path of self-creation? Before choosing, you need to see clearly the risks and benefits associated with either choice.

If you choose to conform to current society and let it, and those who are under its thrall, tell you how to live, you will save yourself the hard work of answering life's questions for yourself. You will fit in and be acceptable to the vast majority of people in this country who have made the same choice as you have and are therefore doing the same things you are. You will have achieved what all of us instinctively need: the acceptance of other people. But you will have done so at a terrible price.

The price is the loss to yourself and to society of who you really are and what you could have become had you taken yourself seriously. You will belong, but you will live without integrity and purpose. Your life will have been wasted in mindless consumerism, inevitably leading to ennui, and possibly depression.

If, on the other hand, you decide to take yourself seriously, and use your brain to determine what you are made of and what use can be put to what you discover—as opposed to option one where you use your brain to be the first on your block to follow the latest trend—you have chosen the harder path. If you choose to create your own life rather than accept one ready-made from someone else, you risk losing friends, friends who are threatened by you because you remind them of what they could have become had they not taken (in order to be included, or not to be excluded) the easier route. Furthermore, you will have to live with the uncertainty of what the outcome will be of living a life of your own making. There is no telling beforehand where it will take you. It's a remote possibility, but could not such a journey take you to a remote cabin in the wilderness, surrounded only by wild animals?

This, I believe, is the greatest fear of those who choose not to follow the herd—that not only will there not be a crowd around them when they "arrive," but no-one at all! It has been my experience, however, that those who have chosen to create their own lives as they see fit, draw to themselves all the people they need. And those drawn to them like them for being **just who they are**, and encourage more of the same.

Real people struggle to live the real lives they were meant to live. What's not to like? In contrast, how can one form an attachment to a facade created by someone for the purpose of tricking as many people as possible into liking him or her? Who can love a facade? Perhaps the greatest benefit of taking yourself seriously is that the life you create is one designed to fit only one person—you. Such a life draws from you what you were born to give. It is a life lived with purpose and even a sense of mission.

Remember Bill, Anne, and Mary who are at a point in their lives that concepts such as lovable, capable, and fit-for-life are irrelevant. Such concepts are based on comparisons to other people. Those who choose to live by their own lights are beyond such comparisons. They are like artists compelled by something inside of them to bring to life something new, something that has never been before. There is no boredom here, no question of "is this all there is." There is only excitement, energy, focus and commitment.

You know and admire people like this. You can become one of them. I believe that you **want** to become one of them. Why? You wouldn't have read this far if you didn't want to.

So, once you have shed who you are not, and determine to find who you are, what's your next step?

CHAPTER 14

Who are you, really?

In order to find out who you are, what the world is like (including the world of work), and where you best fit in that world, you must first understand the nature of people and of the world.

People

Everyone is different than everyone else. Even identical twins born to the same family, going to the same school will be different in the end because they, at birth, have different temperaments, different souls and different gifts (even those with identical gifts possess different **portions** of each gift) to be used in the world. Additionally, each one of the pair will have different experiences in the family, at school, and in society that will form the context in which his temperament, soul and gifts will be expressed.

It is the initial task of individuals to use the qualities only human beings possess—the ability to reason, to plan, to imagine, to learn, to compare, to choose, to anticipate, etc.—to figure out who they are and what makes them the same as, and different than other people.

The World

The next task of individuals is to use their human qualities to figure out the nature of the world, of life itself. First of all, he must learn how to preserve the life he has in that world: cars can kill—look and listen before you cross a street; fire burns; jumping from tree limbs over ten feet from the ground can break your legs, etc.

Secondly, he must learn the tasks required of living independently from his parents: the relevant content of subjects in school; personal finances; the skills of doing for yourself what your mother and father once did for you; the nature of the job market in this country as well as how to get and hold a job, etc.

Finally, if he intends to live happily and with purpose, he must answer for himself the existential questions that face us all: Who am I; Why am I here; What is life all about; Where am I going; How can I best use myself in my short time here.

You can plainly see how clear and accurate answers to these questions are necessary for one to find and take his proper place in the world. The key is to find **your** place, not just **any** place. The difference between finding your place in the world and any place is comparable to the difference between living and surviving, and photographs in color as opposed to black-and-white.

Types

Does the fact that everyone is different mean that one can make no generalizations about who you are and where you best fit in the world, that everyone starts completely from scratch? No. It has been my experience that, although different, people are sufficiently similar to be identified as having one of four personality types. One's personality type is a combination of all of one's important traits that cause one to approach life in a characteristic way. The types are illustrated in Figure 1, the Life Orientation Pie (from page 7 of *What's Your Career*).

LIFE ORIENTATION PIE

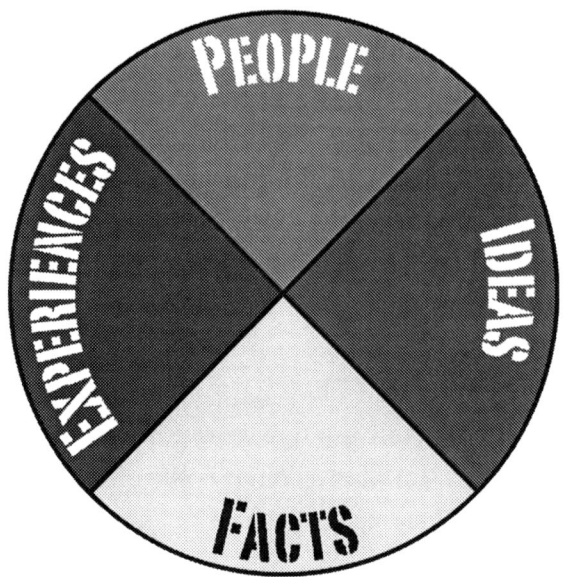

People

There are two sub-types of *People* people: There are those who are interested in individual human beings and their needs, and those who are interested in the human experience and life itself.

Those with an individual focus tend to arrange their lives in such a way that they are in close, intimate contact with people. They are usually involved in occupations that offer care for human individuals by addressing (or helping them to address) their physical, vocational, mental, emotional and spiritual needs. Those who look at life from this point of view are, for example, doctors, teachers, clergy, and psychologists.

Those with a more universal, human-experience focus tend to live lives that revolve in some way around living or human life: pondering it, exploring it, looking at it in unconventional ways, and then illustrating their understandings in artistic manners. Their aim is to, first, immerse themselves in the stuff of life, to feel what it is like to so do, and then to express that feeling in their medium of choice. Those who look at life from this point of view are, for example, actors, writers, and painters

Facts

Those with a *Facts* orientation or type are interested in being part of a group which is organized to perform some sort of task or accomplish some sort of goal. As such, they seek to become proficient in the use of the prevalent knowledge, procedures, and tools of the day to achieve personal, governmental, and organizational goals. Those who look at life from this point of view are, for example, politicians, entrepreneurs, office workers, and workers in the skilled trades and/or crafts.

Experiences

Those with an *Experiences* orientation or type tend to arrange their lives in such a way that they encounter the essence—the elemental nature—of the things of life for no other reason than to know the sensations of direct experience, unfiltered by human invention. If they were interested in experiencing, say, ranch life in the American West, they would sign on as ranch hands on a real, working ranch rather than contract for two weeks at a dude ranch. Those who look at life from this point of view are, for example, farmers, athletes and cops.

Ideas

While those with an *Experiences* orientation or type would probably be content to just experience something, as it is, those with an *Ideas* orientation probably would not. They would more likely undertake to understand why the experience happened in the first place, and why they reacted to it as they did; they might even try to quantify it. They tend to be seekers of knowledge using insight, theories, hypotheses, and experimentation to find objective "truth" or to solve practical problems. Those who look at life from this point of view are, for example, philosophers, physicists, and anthropologists.

Having just rid yourself, in the previous section, of what you are not, you are free to look at yourself anew, this time with clear, unbiased, and more realistic eyes. Study the descriptions of the four life orientations or types. Which sound like you? Your true preferences may be found way back in your past, before you found it necessary to cover your true self with a false, but acceptable, reality. Who, after all, has to tell a baby that it is fun to suck on just about anything? A baby instinctively, intuitively knows it is. Who has to tell a 4-year-old boy or girl that it is pleasurable to run? Each knows instinctively and intuitively that it is.

Your instincts and intuition are still intact and, furthermore, are no longer inhibited by the habitual actions and ways of being you have picked up from your culture. From that natural, unencumbered place where your instincts and intuition are intact and functioning, read the descriptions again. Which sounds like the new you?

As might be expected, people of different life orientations or types think and act differently, as illustrated in Figure 2, the Life Orientation Pie Wedges chart (from page 8 of *What's Your Career*).

LIFE ORIENTATION PIE WEDGES

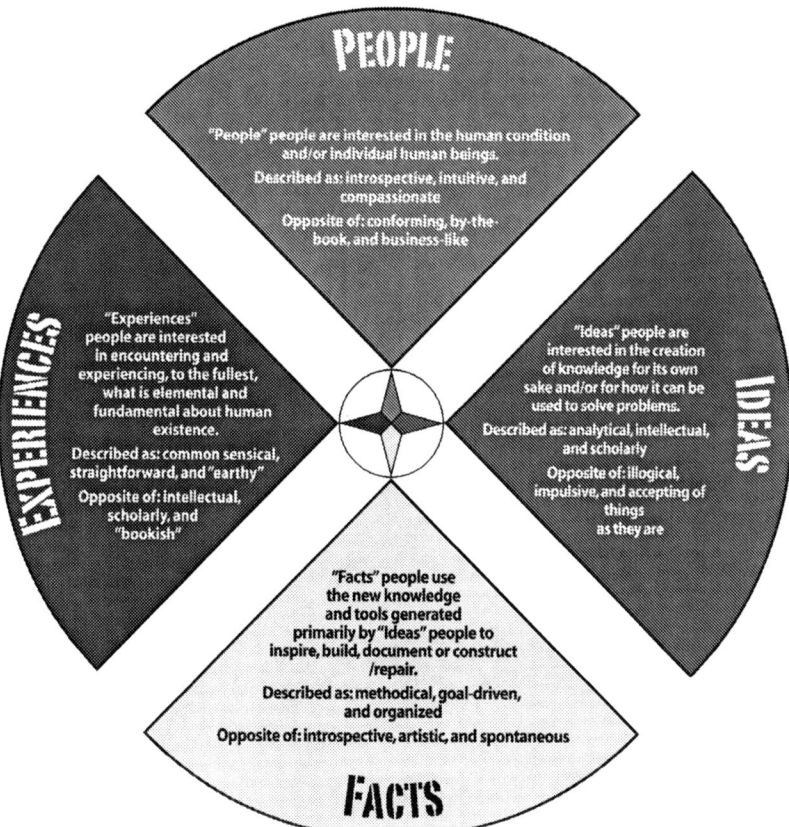

Read the descriptions and their opposites for each orientation/type and answer again: Which sounds like the new, the real you?

But how, you might ask, do personality types or life orientations translate to one's best fit in the world? One more illustration should help: Figure 3, The Heart Zone Pie (from page 15 of *What's Your Career*).

Note that the Heart Zone Pie divides employment in this country into four general categories: Humanitarian, Scientific, Organizational and Natural. These categories correspond to the four life orientations or types discussed earlier. For example, those occupations that call for individuals with a *People* life orientation or type fall into the Humanitarian employment category. Those occupations that call for individuals with an *Ideas* life orientation or type fall into the Scientific category, and so forth.

Furthermore, each general employment category is broken

down into three Heart Zones depicting people who are employed in occupations in which they are engaged in work that feels like play. It is work that exquisitely fits those thus employed. They are not just jobs to them, but outlets for the expression of who they are and what they are here in the world to do.

Once you have explored to a point that you can with confidence choose a pie wedge or, indeed, a pie slice (Heart Zone) that is a good fit for the new you, I recommend you find a high school or college counselor to help you find ways to research specific occupations that fall within your wedge or slice of choice. For those who would prefer to go it alone, a fuller explication of the career system, charts and procedures just described is available at the Educational Media Corporation (see below).

Finally, retrieve the high school picture of yourself that you used throughout the "remembering" process. Next, locate a picture to represent the "you" of today—that is, one that reflects the image of you that best fits the person you want to be, the one you have just discovered and are in the process of becoming. From the objects, pictures and other artifacts you have used to this point, retrieve those that will help you paint a picture of this vital, grounded, engaged, and connected individual.

Now, locate pictures, objects or anything else that suggest to you the place you want to go, from where you are now. It may be a picture of someone who is happily employed in an occupation and life that you aspire to. It may be an object that reminds you of a time in your life when you were most optimistic, hopeful and forward-looking. It may be a picture that you draw or paint that captures the spirit of the person you have always dreamed of being, that you now consider within the realm of possibility.

Arrange all these things around the high school picture of you and the "now" picture of you in a way that makes sense to you. This is the dream that you are now going to create in reality. This is the life you will happily and zestfully pursue and eventually inhabit from this time on.

Take a picture of the tableau you thus create. For inspiration, stick it to your refrigerator. This is the blueprint to you new life!

How motivated are you to do the hard, but exciting work that I've laid out for you here? I guess it comes down to how important it is to you that, in the short time that you have here on earth, you live **your** life—a life that you conceive of and create based on your own inner urgings—rather than someone else's.

For a check on how much of the authentic "you" that you acknowledge as yourself, **to** yourself, do Exercise 4.

Exercise 4

What is your estimate of the percentage of what you know as "yourself" is your "real" self—that is, that part of you that comes from your true, internal nature as opposed to being imposed upon you by others or adopted by you from the "outside":

>   0
> |
>   15
> |
>   30
> |
>   45
> |
>   60
> |
>   75
> |
>   90
> |
>   *100*

If you are like me, your score on this scale will, at first, disappoint you and, then, motivate you to do better. It is very hard to turn away from society's assurance of acceptance, albeit with the cost of your willingness to comply with its dictates. It's equally hard to turn from the safety of acceptance to the uncertainty of the search for yourself and the hope of authenticity. So, I'm continually distressed by my low score on this exercise. At the same time, though, I am usually heartened that it is higher than the last time I did it. In other words, I'm making slow, but steady progress. I expect you'll do the same.

There is another exercise I use to monitor my progress toward authenticity. It provides a reading on how much of what I now present to the world is really "me"—Exercise 5. Whereas I do Exercise 4 every three months or so, I do Exercise 5 weekly, if not daily, when I hit rough patches.

Exercise 5

What percentage of "you," the real you, do you allow other people around you to see (as opposed to the much more acceptable, but false, person you **want** them to see)?

0
|
15
|
30
|
45
|
60
|
75
|
90
|
100

These two exercises should do for you what they do for me. They keep me honest and on track!

CONCLUSION

With this book, you have gone from high school impressions, pretty much imposed upon you by others and accepted blindly, to living a life based solely upon internal urgings, a life based on a true reading of who you are and where you belong, regardless of what others say or what the culture "recommends." You are free to be who you want to be, listening to the voice coming from deep inside you that was lost to you for a time, but has now been recovered.

Not everyone will be pleased that you have decided to "figure it all out" for yourself rather than wait for someone else to hand it to you, ready-made. You will lose some friends, maybe close friends, and there will be those who don't like what you become. But some will; the very ones you need—those who love you for the beautiful person that you are, deep down, and who will encourage and help you to be more of "you" every day.

Your journey may take you to places you weren't even aware existed. On the other hand, the outward circumstances of your life—your job, your family, your home, your friends—may change little. But **you** will have changed in attitude and your approach to your life, because you now know that your life was freely chosen by you and not adopted wholesale from someone or something from the "outside."

Kate Mulgrew, who portrayed Captain Kathryn Janeway in the television series "Star Trek:Voyager," referring to her work as the Captain and her personal life during the seven-year run of the show, states that she "used herself well." I hope that this book helps you to use yourself well. I'm convinced that if enough of us use ourselves well, we will transform the world.

Bill, Anne, and Mary created and are courageously and joyously living lives they love. I hope and trust that you, too, will discover and take very, very seriously that wonderful person you call, "Me!"

> *Note that this book stands alone (that is, without the tools employed in the alternative half of Part 2 of the book) and has been used successfully by many people to create lives they love. Others have found it useful to include, in their quest for a new, more authentic existence, the following tools created by Dr. Ekbom and sold by Educational Media Corporation: *What's Your Story* (2001) and *What's Your Career* (2003).

PART 2

How about you?

Alternative Two: to be read by those who have What's Your Story and What's Your Career.

CHAPTER 9

Comparisons

*Note that, throughout the rest of the book, I will be referring to two counseling tools I developed previously that you will be using when examining your own life—What's Your Story (WYS) and What's Your Career (WYC). Be familiar with them before you start this section.

What do these three people have to do with you and your life? After all, you are grown-up, respected, and successful. Well, all I can say to you is that however "grown-up" you are, there lives within you the child you were. Furthermore, some of the childhood decisions you made about who you were and what was possible for you also still live in you and affect you today.

Do you doubt me? Have you ever gone "home" to your parent's house for the holidays and found yourself acting like the child or sibling you once were? Have you ever attended a high school reunion and observed yourself, and your classmates, revert to the roles you all played when you were in high school? Have you ever found yourself suddenly transported to a previous time in your life at an unsuspected sound, sight, or smell?

I like the story of the young husband who, after a Sunday meal of roast ham, idly asked his wife why she always cut the ends off her ham roasts. The wife replied that that was the way her mother always did it. Curious now herself, she called her mother and asked her why she always cut her ham in this way. Her reply: because her pan was too small to do otherwise! Another example of automatic action, from the past, without conscious thought. How many of our actions have similar origins—automatic, unconscious, from the past and, like the ham story, off the mark? Keep in mind that conclusions drawn and beliefs set, **no matter when formed**, usually stay alive and active unless re-examined and changed in light of present reality.

Since beliefs drive behaviors, if your beliefs are faulty, your behaviors will also be faulty—that is, your decisions will be based on false information, leading to unanticipated, probably unwanted consequences. Keep in mind that most people tend to forget their past as they grow up, not knowing that decisions made then about who they are and what they can become, affect them today. If they are not happy as adults, chances are the source of their unhappiness is trying to live in the present based on faulty conceptualizations from the past.

That's what therapy is all about: going back in time, looking at old beliefs formed at a time when you were a dependent child who had little facility to judge the accuracy of the information you were taking in from your environment. Unless those beliefs have been revisited in adulthood, chances are good that they still live in you today. In therapy one looks, with an adult mind, at faulty beliefs formed in childhood with the aim of replacing them with beliefs that conform to one's present, adult reality.

I've also found that "success" in this country is a slippery concept. I have encountered many people who, by all outward appearances—power, prestige, money, possessions, etc.—are what most people and society would call successful, but deem themselves unhappy and discontent. Imagine struggling mightily for and finally possessing all that society has to offer and finding, in the end, not happiness but instead that "is this all there is" feeling. If you have everything that society holds dear and it does not make you happy, does that mean there is something wrong with society, or with you? Where does one go from there?

Are you successful? Maybe the better question is, are you happy? Most people answer this question with something like: "Well, I'm not unhappy, but I can't say I'm happy either." Many of us are familiar with the "is this all there is" feeling, suspecting that there is "something more" for us out there, but don't know where to find it. The more contemplative of us realize that the "more" is not to be found by looking outside ourselves into the world but inward, within ourselves. So let's take an inward look.

Let's begin by taking a reading of your **present** life perspective. Keeping in mind the definitions provided previously in this book, complete these exercises as best you can, from your present point of view:

Exercise 1

Am I <u>lovable</u>: evidence for this?

          +   = <u>Adequate/Fit for life</u>

Am I <u>capable</u>: evidence for this?

At what level are you adequate/fit for life?

Explain:

1) adequate, a creator of my own life (Grower)
2) adequate, an efficient follower (Adjuster)
3) adequate, as long as nothing changes (Survivor)

Based on your answers to Exercise 1, answer the 3 vital life questions:

Exercise 2

    Who am I?

    What's the world like?

    What's my place in the world?

Exercise 3

Where would you place yourself on the following scales?

Attractiveness	Intelligence	Careers
Brad Pitt/ Angelina Jolie	Albert Einstein/ Margaret Thatcher	Doctor/Lawyer
|	|	|
|	|	|
|	|	|
|	|	|
|	|	|
|	|	|
|	|	|
|	|	|
|	|	|
Ernest Borgnine/ Ruth Buzzi	Three Stooges/ Edith Bunker	Hamburger flipper

Now, take the "people" cards from the WYS pouch and select those that will allow you to recreate your birth family as you remember it. From the "places" stack of cards take out the "school" card. Let that represent your school when you were growing up. You may want to use more of the "place" cards to recreate the town/city in which you grew up. Pick from the "people" cards those that can represent classmates, teachers and good friends (chums) who were around you and important to you when you were about to graduate from high school. Finally, pick a card to represent yourself at that time in your life. In choosing the cards for this and subsequent readings, remember that they are caricatures that need not look just like you or anyone else in order to be effective. As long as something in the card strongly reminds you of the person or place portrayed—clothes, hair, expression, colors, shapes, etc.—they are sufficient for the purpose intended.

Next, on a table with lots of room, arrange all these cards, in a way that makes sense to you, around the card you chose to represent yourself. You may find it useful to include in the mix some photographs of yourself and your family, as well as a school yearbook or some other artifact that represents "high school" to you. Remember, the object of this exercise is to bring you back in time to the person you were at that place and time.

Focus on the card that represents "you." Allow yourself to see "yourself" in the card. Allow yourself to go back in time and inhabit that person you were then. In your mind, surround yourself with the people, things, and the environment from back then.

Breathe life into the scene. Zero in on your young self in that special place and time; think what you were thinking then, feel what you were feeling then, dream as you did then. Use any of the other figures from all the sets of cards in the pouch (animals, people, moods, weather, places, and abstracts) to allow you to conjure up the world you lived in then and how you felt about yourself and about life in it. Are you there? Good. Now, from the point of view of this young person, do exercises 1, 2, and 3 again.

Most people find quite a difference in their responses to the exercises when answered as the adults they are as opposed to those of the adolescents they were. Why? Because, in the years since high school graduation, they have tested what were merely predictions or assumptions about what **might** happen against reality—what actually **did** happen to them. What proved to be demonstrably false in their early predictions was replaced by reality.

What did you find? If you are like most people, you will

have discovered a variation of: "I feel more comfortable in my own skin. I'm less hard on myself for my 'failures.' I'm more confident that I can 'make it' financially and otherwise in the world, despite frequent changes in the world and the workplace." But, I also hear this: "Despite all this, I'm not as happy as I had hoped to be at this point in my life."

It is my guess that **you** are not as happy as you hoped to be at this point in your life, that what you have gained in understanding about yourself and the world over the years is not enough for you. How do I know this? Because you are reading this book. If you were satisfied with your life as it is, you wouldn't be reading about discovering "the person you were meant to be"; you would be out happily living your life. I surmise that you are experiencing a variation of the "is this all there is" syndrome suffered by the "successful" people described above. If it makes you feel any better, you are not alone. There are a whole lot of people out there, just like you, thinking the same thing but afraid to admit it.

Why? You've worked hard, played the game. Where are the promised rewards in happiness and contentment for a life lived doing what you were supposed to do? Could it be that what you have learned over the years--that has admittedly improved your life, although leaving you wishing for more—constitutes only cosmetic improvements? That is, from high school graduation to now did you merely refine your "moves," learn to play society's game better? Did you get better at adjusting to and accommodating society, but still feel unfulfilled? What if what you're doing now with your "career" and "lifestyle" is merely playing a more sophisticated version of the "please love me" game you played in high school with your classmates? Are you saying to yourself, "there's got to be more than this?"

The good news is that there is, indeed, more than this. But it takes hard work to find it. And "it" is not to be found outside of you, in society, but inside you. And the search begins where it started: in your past.

It has been my professional experience that, in order to grow, one must first remove blocks to growth: faulty conclusions from one's past and beliefs about oneself and the world that are untrue.

Let's start with a closer look at your birth family.

CHAPTER 10

Home

Note: before beginning this chapter read through Step 6 of WYC.

Set aside for a time the "school" and "place" cards and any accompanying artifacts you chose for the previous reading and let's focus on the remaining "home" cards and artifacts. Are your parents there, your siblings? Perhaps you lived with grandparents or pets that were important to you—add them. Using all cards in the WYS pouch that fit the scene, lay out your birth family in a way that makes sense to you. Add some old family pictures. Make sure you include some of you when you were young and "innocent." Include, as well, a Christmas picture where everyone is included and there is a favorite, characteristic pose in it by you. You may want to add some old "stair step" pictures of yourself from kindergarten or thereabouts to the card you chose in the first "reading" that encapsulated "you" as a late adolescent so as to give you a sense of your total, conscious experience in this family.

Again, immerse yourself in the scene. Let yourself, first, remember how it was and then, give it the spark of life and live it again, as best you can. (It helps some people to do this in the company of a trusted friend; the friend can best help by just listening to you, without comment, unless told otherwise).

Focus first on your parents or primary care-givers. Were they in the survival mode, adjustment mode or growth mode, as described above? How did this fact manifest itself in your family?

Now, focus on dad. What was he like then? Describe him in a few words. How would you answer this: "Dad would always say_____." What was his general outlook on life? What was his relationship with your mother? How did he view, treat her? How did he view and treat women in general? Men in general? How did he view, treat his kids? How did he view, treat you?

Do the same with your mother. How did your parents get along, treat one another? How did they parent? Did they set your feet on the path of the growth mode, adjustment mode, or survival mode?

From the scene, choose a favorite family picture—perhaps the Christmas picture. Are these people happy or sad? Why or why not? In the picture, are you happy or sad? Why?

Now focus on the cards and pictures you chose for all your family members. Go over them individually. Tell your friend about all of them, then and now. Where were you in the birth order? How did this affect you? What roles did each take in the family? What was your role? Do you still play that role today, in your family and otherwise?

Finally, focus on your "you" card and a favorite picture of yourself. Tell your friend all about this kid as if the kid was a good friend, rather than yourself: "This is your name. She is ...." What are your feelings towards this kid? Was he/she good/

bad, lovable/unlovable, capable/incapable, worthy of love and caring/unworthy of loving and caring? Explain.

Did you feel loved by dad, by mom, by your siblings? Did you feel that your family treated you with respect? Explain.

After you are deeply into your feelings about yourself and your family at this time in your life, ask yourself the following questions:

- If you felt disrespected or mistreated by your father, did you conclude (with your child mind), that you were unworthy of respect?

- If you felt second-best in comparison to your siblings in the eyes of your mother, did your conclude (with your child mind) that your were unlovable?

- If your family was too large for your parents to give you the individual attention you needed, did you conclude (with your child mind) that you were insignificant?

- If your oldest sister was the "beauty queen" of the school, did you (with your child mind) conclude that you were ugly?

- If your older brother, whom you considered your best friend, went off to college and "forgot" you, did you conclude (with your child mind) that you were forgettable?

- If your mother and father split up when you were a child, did you conclude (with your child mind), that it was your fault?

- If you were put up for adoption because your parent/parents couldn't/wouldn't take care of you, did you conclude (with your child mind), that there was something wrong with you and no-one would want you?

- If your father wanted you to fulfill a dream in the world that he couldn't, did you (with your child mind) conclude that you had to do it for him, or you wouldn't be a "good" son?

- If your parents believed that boys were more "valuable" than girls, and you're a girl, did you conclude (with your child mind), that all boys were more valuable than you were?
- Add any others that came to you as you were time-traveling in the "previous time" exercise above and/or that occur to you now:

If ...., did you conclude (with your child mind) that.....................?

These, and uncountable other false, yet limiting beliefs are what cause us to think less of ourselves than we are, and constrict our dreams. While feeling the hurt that still exists from these old, yet familiar beliefs, stand up to them and, with your adult mind, dispute the truth of them. For example: Isn't it true--and you can see it clearly now that you are an adult—that your father had no respect to give because he didn't respect himself? Your resulting belief--a belief that is as true for you today as it was then--that you are unworthy of respect, is incorrect. So what is correct? Are you worthy of respect? Why? You may, now, also have to reevaluate how you feel about your father. He may no longer be, in your mind, the personification of evil (or virtue) you always thought he was—but, on the other hand, he'll probably be more human to you. And your self-respect will rise. Chances are too that, after a time, your relationship with him will improve.

In this simulation, what did you learn about yourself, life and where you might fit in life? Share these feelings and thoughts with your friend. Acknowledge and make friends with the vulnerable, yet precious child that still lives in you today.

How did what you concluded about yourself and the world when you were a vulnerable and dependent child affect how you answered the lovable/capable questions above? What burdens from your past do you carry to this day? Are there things of value that you've always had, but forgotten about that you need to recover and use? Are there things that you carry that are no longer true or useful (if they ever were) that you want to let go?

CHAPTER 11

School and other people

I have found that, like one's birth family, one's K-12 schooling has a great impact on how a person feels about himself and his future prospects in the world. Family is understandable, as demonstrated in Chapter 11. What is it, though, about early schooling?

I believe one's first school experience is so impactful because it's a person's initiation into the outer world, where one encounters ideas and ways of being that are different from what one has learned at home. I think, too, it's important because one realizes that it is in this setting, without the protection of one's family and in the company of these strange "others" that the bulk of one's life will be lived and one must sink or swim with them.

It is the first setting in which one has to choose whom to believe--parents or peers and the popular culture with which they are imbued. Furthermore, people outside one's family don't **have** to love you because you are "family." "Outsiders," therefore, will love you or not based on your merits, or lack thereof. Finally, it's at school that kids are, in effect, ranked according to their grades. Many kids with a 2.0 grade point average in school resign themselves to a 2.0 future.

Throw in the strong feelings and emotions associated with physical maturing and you have the ingredients of a strong brew, boiling away. Balancing these powerful influencers, some of which undoubtedly sending opposite messages, one takes his first tentative steps toward a personal philosophy. That is why conclusions drawn, and beliefs established at this tumultuous time of life tend to set one's mode of feeling, thinking, and acting that, unless seriously challenged in some way—be it chance events, natural maturing, or therapy—will remain throughout one's life.

Set aside the "home" pictures, cards and artifacts for the time being and retrieve the "school" card. Scan the card deck for any images that whisper "high school" to you. From the deck, choose cards to represent important teachers, administrators (both good and bad), good friends and bad enemies, as well as the card you've chosen to represent yourself. Complete the scene with any pictures, yearbooks, or mementos that can help you get in the mood to go back in time. I recommend that you have a close friend, perhaps even an old classmate, with you as you reminisce, and with whom you can share your old triumphs and hurts. Some people find it useful, prior to this session, to visit their old school. Arrange the cards and accessories in a way that makes sense to you.

Begin with your "you" card and a favorite picture of yourself in a school setting around graduation time, one that personifies what you thought about yourself and about life in general at this time in your life. What about this kid? What is he/she wearing? What is the setting? What is he/she thinking/feeling in this picture? Tell this all to your trusted friend. In detail, describe this kid, yourself, to your friend as if the kid was someone close that you used to know very well. Now, immerse yourself in this young person and his/her world, as you did with your family above. Once "there," ask:

- If your best friend moved away before you graduated and you never saw or heard from him/her again, did you conclude (with your child mind) that it hurts too badly to get too close to people?

- If you were a bone-head in math, did you conclude (with your child mind) that you were stupid?

- If you were always chosen last for games in PE class, did you conclude (with your child mind) that you were not physically competitive and would have to rely on your brain alone to get along in the world? No marathons for you?

- If you were targeted by a bully who told you that you were fat and ugly, did you conclude (with your child mind) that you were, indeed, fat and ugly and therefore bad?

- If you were dating a variety of boys to see what kind of boys there were out there and, consequently, were told by some that you were a "slut," did you conclude (with your child mind) that you were, indeed, a slut?

- If you slept with a lot of girls in high school and your buddies, in consequence, called you a "stud," did you conclude (with your child mind) that you were, indeed, a stud?

- If you were "smarter" than most of your classmates, did you conclude (with your child mind) that you were better than they were, too?

- If you were intimately acquainted with the principal's office, did you conclude (with your child mind) that you were "one bad dude."

- If you fell in love with one of your teachers and she married another man, did you conclude (with your child mind), that you would never love another woman? (I did that. It turned out not to be true!)

- Add others relevant to your situation:

If ...., did you conclude (with your child mind) that............

Again, feel the hurt, and then express the hurt to your friend (whom you've instructed to just listen, no matter what you say or do—unless asked to do differently). With your adult mind, dispute the truth of your early conclusions. With the bullying example above, realize that the bully was a troubled kid; he probably thought that **he** was ugly and was trying to deal with the pain of this by attacking you.

Again, looking at a picture of yourself taken at that time, ask yourself, as if looking at someone other than yourself: "Is this kid fat and ugly?" And, "Do I consider myself fat and ugly, now?" And, finally: "Have I held myself hostage to this boy all these years?"

Consider the impact of holding such a belief might have had, and continues to have, on your self-esteem, your perceived fitness for life and subsequent life choices.

CHAPTER 12

Society

Society, or one's culture, is so big, so ever-present, so insistent that it is hard to resist its dictates. And dictate it does. Through advertisements, companies want to convince you that you will not fit or belong with your contemporaries if you do not buy their products. Movies and magazines present to us the "ideal" male and female in looks, attitudes, and behaviors. Once indoctrinated with its dictates, "citizens" like us tend to re-indoctrinate one another until it seems that the only way to avoid being an outcast is to conform to society's ever-changing demands. And it is in this environment that we know, even at age 18, that we must prepare ourselves for careers and for marriage and families.

Set aside you school cards and materials and retrieve the ones you chose to represent your town or city. Let them represent for you the world or life as you knew it as an 18-year-old. Put the card in the mix that you choose to represent yourself. You might have stored away pictures of you with your best friend/friends at this vital time in your life—add them. It might help to visit your old home town and, perhaps, answer some of these questions with a group of old classmates. Again, pictures, cards and other artifacts have a way of helping people take themselves back in time so they are not just reminiscing, but actually re-living earlier times. Find some that remind you of the times you lived as a budding adolescent. Some people find it helpful to add to the mix pictures from magazines that were popular in those days. When you are "in character," answer the following:

- If you saw most of the people around you smoking, did you conclude (with your child mind) that you must smoke, too, in order to not be excluded?

- Did you conclude (with your child mind) that those people who most closely resembled the "teen idols" of the time, were better than those who didn't, like yourself?

- If your grades were just "ok" in high school, did you conclude (with your child mind) that you could only hope for an "ok" kind of job and life?

- If your family could not afford the clothes and accessories that most other kids were wearing in school, did you conclude (with your child mind) that they were better than you?

- When you observed that towns-people with white-collar occupations seemed to have more money and prestige than those with blue-collar occupations, did you (with your child mind) conclude that white-collar people are better than blue collar people?

- Did you conclude (with your child mind) that children of white-collar parents were better than the children of blue-collar people?

- Add other scenarios relevant to your situation:

If……………………………, did you conclude (with your child mind) that ……………

Again, allow yourself to feel the hurt that may arise in you as a result of this exercise. Express your hurt to your friend or friends. Now, consider with your adult mind, whether or not any of it is true. More importantly, whether objectively true or not, did you believe it to be true, and live as if it were true? Do you today?

Consider the impact on your present life of holding untruths, as truths. Remember, society or other people can only hurt you if you believe the nasty things they are saying to you, about you. As a child, you may have felt that you had no choice but to believe; as an adult, you do.

Do you feel better? Lighter? Freer? Have you realized, yet, that your negative thoughts about yourself were the result of your own faulty conclusions, based on child-like reasoning? Have you realized that the greatest barrier to a better, more meaningful life for yourself has been, and remains, yourself? Do you realize that you do not have to compare yourself to other people and that the only meaningful, useful comparison to be made is between who you are now and who you could be? Do you realize that no court in the land is going to prosecute you if you choose to live a life of your own choosing, one that is different than that of most others? Do you realize that you are not a freak of nature, less than other people, boring, insignificant, unworthy of the good things in life? Do you realize that you are the way you are for a reason?

Do you realize that you are okay, just the way you are if you'll but **be** who you are?

CHAPTER 13

Take your pick

What you have done to this point, is purge yourself of what you are not. You have started thinking for yourself rather than passively accepting what other people and your culture say you are and/or should be. What this means for you is that you have recovered the power of choice. Other people or entities no longer have the power to make your choices for you, unless you consciously let them do so. So what will you do with this new freedom? What will you choose: the easy route of passively following society's dictates, or the much more difficult, but infinitely more gratifying path of self-creation? Before choosing, you need to see clearly the risks and benefits associated with either choice.

If you choose to conform to current society and let it, and those who are under its thrall, tell you how to live, you will save yourself the hard work of answering life's questions for yourself. You will fit in and be acceptable to the vast majority of people in this country who have made the same choice as you have and are therefore doing the same things you are. You will have achieved what all of us instinctively need: the acceptance of other people. But you will have done so at a terrible price.

The price is the loss to yourself and to society of who you really are and what you could have become had you taken yourself seriously. You will belong, but you will live without integrity and purpose. Your life will have been wasted in mindless consumerism, inevitably leading to ennui, and possibly depression.

If, on the other hand, you decide to take yourself seriously, and use your brain to determine what you are made of and what use can be put to what you discover—as opposed to option one where you use your brain to be the first on your block to follow the latest trend—you have chosen the harder path. If you choose to create your own life rather than accept one ready-made from someone else, you risk losing friends, friends who are threatened by you because you remind them of what they could have become had they not taken (in order to be included, or not to be excluded) the easier route. Furthermore, you will have to live with the uncertainty of what the outcome will be of living a life of your own making. There is no telling beforehand where it will take you. It's a remote possibility, but could not such a journey take you to a remote cabin in the wilderness, surrounded only by wild animals?

This, I believe, is the greatest fear of those who choose not to follow the herd—that not only will there not be a crowd around them when they "arrive," but no-one at all! It has been my experience, however, that those who have chosen to create their own lives as they see fit, draw to themselves all the people they need. And those drawn to them like them for being **just who they are**, and encourage more of the same.

Real people struggle to live the real lives they were meant to live. What's not to like? In contrast, how can one form an attachment to a facade created by someone for the purpose of tricking as many people as possible into liking him or her? Who can love a facade? Perhaps the greatest benefit of taking yourself seriously is that the life you create is one designed to fit only one person--you. Such a life draws from you what you were born to give. It is a life lived with purpose and even a sense of mission.

Remember Bill, Anne, and Mary who are at a point in their lives that concepts such as lovable, capable, and fit-for-life are irrelevant. Such concepts are based on comparisons to other people. Those who choose to live by their own lights are beyond such comparisons. They are like artists compelled by something inside of them to bring to life something new, something that has never been before. There is no boredom here, no question of "is this all there is." There is only excitement, energy, focus and commitment.

You know and admire people like this. You can become one of them. I believe that you **want** to become one of them. Why? You wouldn't have read this far if you didn't want to.

So, once you have shed who you are not, and determine to find who you are, what's your next step?

CHAPTER 14

Who are you, really?

Note: for this chapter, read and do the exercises from Step 7 in WYC to the end.

You can choose to focus your brain outward to determine how others want you to live and follow their dictates as closely as possible. Or you can choose to focus your brain inward in order to figure out who you are and where and with whom you best fit. If you choose the latter, read on!

With WYC, you will first discover which of the four human "essences," or Life Orientations best describes you. Here you will find people like you, whose life orientation is similar to your own. Are you a People, Facts, Ideas, or Experiences person? With further study of yourself and your natural "clan," you will develop your own personal "Statement of Essence":

"I am the kind of person who is _____ and who needs _____ in my work life in order to be happy."

From there, you are introduced to career interest areas and, finally, specific career paths or "Heart Zones" associated with the interest areas. You go on to match your statement of essence to specific heart zones, described as "areas of employment occupied by men and women whose whole selves are involved in performing the tasks that make up the work—not just their heads, but also their hearts." The idea is to help you match who you are, deep down, with what you're here to do--your inborn "occupation." Along the way, you will meet people so employed in what is described as "core" or "soul" work. Finally, you will explore on the internet specific occupations that match your essence and personality so that you too can find meaning and purpose in what you do.

How motivated are you to do the hard, but exciting work that I've laid out for you here? I guess it comes down to how important it is to you that, in the short time that you have here on earth, you live "your" life--a life that you conceive of and create based on your own inner urgings—rather than someone else's.

For a check on how much of the authentic "you" that you acknowledge as yourself, **to** yourself, do Exercise 4.

Exercise 4

What is your estimate of the percentage of what you know as "yourself" is your "real" self—that is, that part of you that comes from your true, internal nature as opposed to being imposed upon you by others or adopted by you from the "outside":

0
|
15
|
30
|
45
|
60
|
75
|
90
|
100

If you are like me, your score on this scale will, at first, disappoint you and, then, motivate you to do better. It is very hard to turn away from society's assurance of acceptance, albeit with the cost of your willingness to comply with its dictates. It's equally hard to turn from the safety of acceptance to the uncertainty of the search for yourself and the hope of authenticity. So, I'm continually distressed by my low score on this exercise. At the same time, though, I am usually heartened that it is higher than the last time I did it. In other words, I'm making slow, but steady progress. I expect you'll do the same.

There is another exercise I use to monitor my progress toward authenticity. It provides a reading on how much of what I now present to the world is really "me"—Exercise 5. Whereas I do Exercise 4 every three months or so, I do Exercise 5 weekly, if not daily, when I hit rough patches.

Exercise 5

What percentage of "you," the real you, do you allow other people around you to see (as opposed to the much more acceptable, but false, person you **want** them to see)?

```
   0
   |
  15
   |
  30
   |
  45
   |
  60
   |
  75
   |
  90
   |
 100
```

These two exercises should do for you what they do for me. They keep me honest and on track!

CONCLUSION

With this book, you have gone from high school impressions, pretty much imposed upon you by others and accepted blindly, to living a life based solely upon internal urgings, a life based on a true reading of who you are and where you belong, regardless of what others say or what the culture "recommends." You are free to be who you want to be, listening to the voice coming from deep inside you that was lost to you for a time, but has now been recovered.

Not everyone will be pleased that you have decided to "figure it all out" for yourself rather than wait for someone else to hand it to you, ready-made. You will lose some friends, maybe close friends, and there will be those who don't like what you become. But some will; the very ones you need—those who love you for the beautiful person that you are, deep down, and who will encourage and help you to be more of "you" every day.

Your journey may take you to places you weren't even aware existed. On the other hand, the outward circumstances of your life—your job, your family, your home, your friends—may change little. But **you** will have changed in attitude and your approach to your life, because you now know that your life was freely chosen by you and not adopted wholesale from someone or something from the "outside."

Kate Mulgrew, who portrayed Captain Kathryn Janeway in the television series "Star Trek:Voyager," referring to her work as the Captain and her personal life during the seven-year run of the show, states that she "used herself well." I hope that this book helps you to use yourself well. I'm convinced that if enough of us use ourselves well, we will transform the world.

Bill, Anne, and Mary created and are courageously and joyously living lives they love. I hope and trust that you, too, will discover and take very, very seriously that wonderful person you call, "Me!"

BIBLIOGRAPHY

Ekbom, C.W. (2001) <u>What's Your Story: A Projective Card Sort for Children and Adults</u>. Educational Media Corporation, Mpls, MN.

Ekbom, C.W. (2003) <u>What's Your Career?</u> Educational Media Corporation, Mpls, MN.

>Educational Media Corporation
>P.O. Box 21311
>Minneapolis, MN 55421-0311
>www.educationalmedia.com
>(763) 781-0088 or (800) 966-3382

Send "*Life Crafting*" to a Friend or Use It in Your Classroom

O **YES**, I want ____ copies of *Life Crafting* at $12.95 each, plus shipping costs.

My check or money order for $_____ is enclosed. Allow 14 days for delivery.

Name_____

Organization_____

Address_____

City/State/Zip_____

Phone_____

E-mail_____

Signature_____

-or-

O **YES**, please send a copy(ies) of *Life Crafting* at $12.95 each, plus shipping costs to the following person(s) and address(es):

Name_____

Address_____

City/State/Zip_____

Signature_____

Please make your check payable to and send your order to:

Clyde W. Ekbom
P.O. Box 505
Lake Nebagamon, WI 54849-0505

Dr. Ekbom's e-mail address:
souldoc1@msn.com

ABOUT THE AUTHOR

Dr. Clyde W. Ekbom—author, psychologist, counselor, coach, conference presenter—recently retired from a 20-year career as a college professor of Psychology/Counselor Education. Before that he was a high school English teacher, school counselor and coach. Before that, he was a soldier in the U.S. Army in Vietnam. He likes to sing, travel, make maple syrup and read. He loves people of all sorts. By the time you read this, he and his family will be living in Northern Minnesota.

CPSIA information can be obtained at www.ICGtesting.com
Printed in the USA
BVOW071929120313

315372BV00002B/156/A

9 781587 368301